# What Influences Your Life

MONAHENG SELLO NELSON

Published by Author, 2023.

While every precaution has been taken in the preparation of this book, the publisher assumes no responsibility for errors or omissions, or for damages resulting from the use of the information contained herein.

WHAT INFLUENCES YOUR LIFE

**First edition. February 16, 2023.**

Copyright © 2023 MONAHENG SELLO NELSON.

ISBN: 979-8215633250

Written by MONAHENG SELLO NELSON.

## *Table of contents*

## —*DEDICATION*—

First and foremost, I want to dedicate this book to my Lord and personal Saviour Jesus Christ. I do acknowledge your influence, love and wisdom toward my inspirational book, without you this book wouldn't have become an authentic remarkable book. Lord amongst them all" —you remain trustworthy and you're rightfully deserve to be honoured. All the *"Praise, Majesty and Glory"* belongs to you. You favour, and grace has influenced me to become influential and understand the vitality of becoming great - so that I will cause an impact to my generation.

- <u>Introduction</u>-

The system of the world we are living in today, is manipulated by two forces darkness and light. As we are here on planet earth, nobody will be able to conduct their lives without being influenced by these two forces.

Keep in mind, darkness is against light. Thus, all the negative challenges we face as humans fight the knowledge of light so that nobody will understand the power and principles of God. This becomes one of the reasons we struggle in many areas in our lives. Now don't allow the darkness to ***"influence"*** your capacity of you mind; remember we are in a war fighting the system of the devil.

In this Generation, we face many factors that manipulate our thoughts and holds us back from the light of God; poverty, money, ownership of things seen, sickness the list is endless. Thus, we must be aware not to be under the influence of darkness. There is a way God wants us to stand in his word and use the sword of the Spirit and instruct all evil to flee from us.

Learn from God and use the ability HE has given unto you to change your world. Don't doubt who you are because nobody is better than you, the influence of this generation does not have domino over your life. Your presents here on planet earth carry your uniqueness full of your personality, you are here to impact something different into the system.

Your journey of life will never be the same as others because you carry a unique anointing. Time limits cannot hold you down, the system of this world is extremely confusing, demanding and destroying; be careful, not to give your personality to the things of this world to influence your Spirit and your mind!

Instead give your attention to the Word of God, because the Word will make you what it talks about. You will always triumph in every area of your life and you will influence your world and change many people, to be productive and fruitful. You are the hope of glory; your life is with a specific purpose to serve. Be different in action, walk, according to your calling in life, it's important to know who you are in life and know where you are going as a person. The biggest question to you is who influences your life here on this planet, is it GOD or the devil? Which kingdom do you represent as you are a living being?

# Chapter 1

# The spiritual world is influential to our life's

We all under the influence of **good** and **evil** as much as there is nobody in between or neutral; as much as there are two kingdoms on planet earth, the kingdom of light and the kingdom of "darkness". The fact of life is nobody can function in both kingdoms, it`s light or darkness. Both kingdoms have different rules, and they operate in different ways. These kingdoms have something in common because they use human body and Spirit to operate on planet earth.

The kingdom of light use **believes** and **faith of** a man to influences the planet earth, as much as the kingdom of darkness use there believes and faith of a man to operate on planet earth. Both kingdoms need the spirit of a man and body to work on earth they don't use animals, but they use humans not dead things to function. The devils need wisdom from the spirit and a body to work evil ways on planet earth, as much as God needs any man to use for his glory.

The **presents** of God within you is **powerful** to make all things possible for the kingdom of light either the kingdom of darkness. If you not in the kingdom of light, then you in the kingdom of darkness. Nobody can be in the kingdom of light and do the things of the kingdom of darkness; and nobody can be in the kingdom of darkness and do the things of the kingdom of light. For anyone that needs to **function** in the kingdom of light need the spirit of God within himself or herself. And in the kingdom of darkness you need a demon, within you to be able to take part in the evil ways of the devil.

There is something important we have on planet earth as humans and that is the freedom of choice. We have choice and we can choose who do we want to listen too! We able to choose things we want to do and the things we don't want to do. We can refuse to do bad or good. It is a choice we have as humans. The choice we have is given to us by God, and we need to choose wisely on who to follow and listen too! The devil does not let anyone to choose for himself or herself, the devil force himself to anyone in any given time. Be careful not to give the devil any opportunity into your life, because his plan is to kill, steal and destroy your future.

The lives we live today as people is under the inspiration of this two kingdoms and influenced by these two kingdoms. These two kingdoms carry power. The power they carry is **capable** to change anyone to be **submissive** under they authority. The truth of the matter is nobody is doing anything he or she wants to do, because both kingdoms they fight to rule over one body at the same time. Be aware that whatsoever you do on planet earth its either inspired, by the kingdom of light or the kingdom of darkness.

Everyone can listen to his or her Spirit and use the power of choice to choose the kingdom he or she wants to follow and be under it. The kingdom of darkness does not give or offer peace, joy, happiness, love, the list is endless. Anyone influenced by the kingdom of darkness he or she is not happy in the Spirit, the person may **appear happy,** but the truth of the matter is nobody can find happiness in the dark world. Everything offered by the devil is not real is temporal and it comes with sorrows.

It's important to have information knowledge about these two kingdoms, and know how do they work, function and rule. As human beings, we must have understanding and information of where we belong so, that we can be wise on our choice as we choose, the right kingdom to function and operate into by using the understanding and wisdom we have in us.

The real factor of life is God exists as much as the devil exits. God wants us as his people to enjoy the gift of life, He has given to us. If you not happy and glad in your life check where you stand with God and in which kingdom you function into! Many people believe if you have lot of money and everything you need that is happiness or that is where happiness comes from! The **true** meaning of life is not the things a man possesses; because the things you have today they don't give you an identity of who you are in the Spirit. Have knowledge and understanding of who you are in the Spirit, because you not just physical body only as flesh and blood. The reality of life is you are the Spirit being, the image of God you are created in His likeness.

**Now let us investigate the meaning of influence; is the power to affect, control or manipulate something or someone; influence is the ability to change the development of fluctuating things such as conduct, thoughts or decisions.**

It`s important to be **aware** of how information manipulate the decisions we take on our dearly life's. A decision you take today is based on the knowledge you have as a person on the particular subject or on something happening around you at that time. On the other hand your choice of choosing is conduct by your thoughts.

Now! Let us get into more details on how we are influenced in our daily life's, by the things we do and things we **desire** to have as human being. It`s important to know what controls your life; it maybe a passion you have towards an object, or the love you have towards someone special in your life. Most time in life, we fail to work on becoming something, but we work on having things that is where we make our first mistake.

As a person desire to be something, let the spirit man lead you into a right direction you must go. Many people they don`t know what they carry inside them, in you there is a **"spirit man"** that carry all the answers to each and everything that pertain unto life. Sometimes we let our emotions to influence our desire rather letting our desire to influence and control our emotions. I have a strong believe that everyone is meant to do something different with his or her life.

As a human being; never allow the influence of **poverty** to manipulate your present time and the future. Poverty is a location or is the state of mind, first Poverty have a language and it can say things to anyone that listen to it. Poverty have a bad impacted on people and a negative language the is nothing good that precede out of poverty; be careful in your logic that poverty does not manipulate your thoughts and make you to think that without good education your life will never be productive and fruitful.

What makes you different is the power and ability you have inside of you. All things you desire in life you already have them, for the sake you desire them is a confirmation that you have them, and they belong to you. So what poverty does to you it open your eyes and show you the things you don't have and reveal time, processes and the journey you must travel to get everything you are looking for! All challenges you will face then poverty will start to say to you it is impossible to have all this things because of the lack of resource you don't have as a person.

As we are given a gift of life don't allow poverty to influence your tomorrow; and don't let your dreams, good thoughts, and goals to be manipulated by poverty. Allow the desire of good deeds to influence your mind and future: see the impossible, possible use the power within you and manufacture ideas and work towards your ideas and become something in life.

## *TRANSFORM YOUR MIND*

The primary standard of transformation is through the word of God. Basic information it can be used, also on mind transformation. What is important on mind transformation is the "**character**", that is produce through the information allowed on mind and thoughts.

The information we allow into our minds, influence us and form a character based on information given to us; poverty, money, clothes, and cars the list is endless all these objects carry energy and information at the same time they are very active.

In the processes of mind transformation we need to understand three things.

- How does mind transformation take place?
- What are the things we need to be conscious of?

- The character we become, as we are transforming is it a right character for the future?

How does mind transforming take place? First, transformation take place in your thoughts; then goes to your mind and to your spirit to give information to your personality.

Which are the things we need to be conscious of, information we receive is the first primary standard of our conscious. Things we see in our daily lives play a big role, because of the pictures they paint in our imaginations.

After we have received information into our Spirits, what kind of character do we turn to be? We all need to ask ourselves this question, did I turn to be good and productive person with a new character? If the question is not answered, then we know where we can find our answer in the **word of God** the word of God will build us up and gives us a good character.

A true transformation comes from the word of God, the **ability** we have as humans does not have the right capacity to change any person **soul.** Only, the word of God with power and wisdom can renewing the person inner man. The mistake we do, as people is to look on material things of this world to give us transformation. Material things they don't add value or something good into our lives but material things they bring unhappiness, sadness, anger, the list is endless.

The world will give you wrong information make you unhappy, the things a person possess doesn't not add any value unto a person life. Let's go back to the scripture and see what the Holy Spirit says to us about renewing our minds.

The book of (**Romans 12:2KJV**) **and be not conformed by this world: but be ye transformed by the renewing of your mind, that ye may prove what is that good, and acceptable, and perfect, will of God.**

The Spirit of God says it clear to us, that we must not do, think, or act according to the system and standard; of this world but renew our mind through the knowledge of God, so that we can prove the will of the father in heaven. Let's look the word renew what does it mean.

*To make new again to restore to freshness, perfection or vigor; to give new life to; to rejuvenate, to reestablish; to recreate; to rebuild.*

When you allow new information into your life by that you are rebuilding your life on a new information which is the word of God. The word is able to reestablish your life. Renewing your mind is to restoring what you did not have before and adding new experience unto your life. And now, brethren, I commend you to God, and to the word of his grace, which is able to build you up, and to give you an inheritance among all them which are sanctified.(Acts 20:32)

The word of God is the one with ability to build the person up and give the person a new life. The word of God gives a person a inheritances among all them which are sanctified: the is power in the word to change any person character, and give him a new character with new thoughts to renew your mind is to change your thinking and giving yourself new thoughts with a different information; what you used to think about in the past you will no more think about because the Word of God will give you new things to think about and restore your life. (Ephesians 4:23KVJ)**And be renewed in the spirit of your mind**.

For the Word of God to work in your life the word needs you to take part on it and live by it every day and talk about it. Commit yourself on the Word and meditate on it day and night, observe to do according to it and you shall make your way prosperous.

### BE SPIRITUAL MINDED

Everything that exists today is been translated from the spiritual world: there is nothing that just appears by itself here on planet earth. The spiritual world have more influence on the physical world and on the **"material"** things we see with our naked eyes. Let your senses be under the influence of the word of God and your life will be influential, effective and productive every day.

Now let's look at the scriptures and what God says to us; about how we should conduct our lives. And it's important to be spiritually minded with the capacity of the Spirit of God in us, what we carry it reflects to the information we have as humans on planet earth.

Now let's look into the book of *(ROMANS 8:6 KJV) for to be carnally minded is death; but to be spiritually minded is life and peace.*

- First, we got to understand what is *carnality* and its influence.

- Carnality is to have wicked thoughts with negatives imagination.

- Be informed wicked thoughts lead to death.

Let's look at the scripture on top again and understand what the Lord says to us about carnality. Every knowledge that is not of God the information that is against the wisdom and understanding of God is carnality. Now the bible tells us that to be carnally minded is death, and remember we shared above about wicked thoughts lead to death.

- Thoughts and meditation manifest in the physical world.

- Whatsoever negative things we meditate upon as humans the ideas that can bring death.

- Before any person can be able to show anger, wrath, malice, blasphemy, and filthy communication. He or she will have to think towards sure things and a carnally image will be formed within the person heart, then we will see the expression of thoughts he or she was meditating are upon at that moment of time.

● Anything negative that brings shame to the person life is carnality because it have the ability and power of death on it.

The word of God now tells us, **"but to be spiritually minded is life and peace. "**

Every person need life and peace everyday as we go on with our daily life's. First, we need to understand that Christ is our peace and sound mind; thinking about the **sacrificed** Jesus Christ did on the cross giving up His life for us bring peace and life into our Spirit.

Let's go more into details, what kind of life is to be spiritual minded. Following the things of the Spirit and hearing from the Spirit it's life; the mind we must have is the mind of God in our Spirits. The word of God is the mind of God by receiving the *WORD OF GOD* into our hearts the word give us the thoughts of God into our spirits and the light of the Holy Spirit drives out darkness in our imaginations and the peace of God rest upon us. Jesus Christ is our peace, life and without him we can do nothing.

The things of the Spirit how do they influence or manipulate us, into our day to day life's. The word of God is Spirit and alive: the kind of **thoughts** we receive from the Word of God gives us life, and make us capable to do anything we were created for as human being. As individual we able to allow the word of God to give us the thoughts of life and increase. The best thing we are influence by the word of God; and the word of God give us **"direction"** to the life we have to live. The **character** of any individual is under the influence of the information He or she carry within he or herself.

**Let's look in the scripture (Act 20:32KJV) and now, brethren I commend you to God, and to the word of his grace, which is able to**

**build you up, and to give you an inheritance among all them which are sanctified.**

The scripture gives us peace of information with lot of details. First what we find is a commend or instruction: that tells us we are entrust or commit to the care of the **"word"** of God. The second thing we find is **"grace"** that able us to move into worldly system and manipulate the functions of the system. Most important piece of information is the word of God, can and is able to **build us** up to inherit the promises was given to our four fathers.

When the word of God, functions fully into the heart of any person; he or she will realize that inside of him or her there is **ability** to function in the likeness of God. When we are spiritually minded, anything that comes from the **Spirit** will never be a surprise to us, because we carry the mind of God! And function in his likeness.

When we are spiritual minded, it`s easy for us to understand the role we out to play on this planet.

- Being spiritually minded, helps us to understand how to control our emotions and our speech.
- When you are spiritually minded your life will never be ordinary and boring.
- The mind of the spirit will always remind you the purpose that you must serve.
- When you are spiritually minded, you grow fast into maturity and learn the things of the Spirit.
- When you are spiritually minded, you will never do anything without a purpose.
- Being spiritually minded, opens your spiritual eyes to see things before they happen.

I want us to look at the word of God, about the kind of mind Jesus Christ was having as he was here on earth. **(Philippians 2:5 KJV) let this mind be in you, which was also in Christ Jesus.**

Here the Spirit of God spoke through Paul, informing us about the kind of person Jesus was here on planet earth. And also, the kind of things he did as he was on earth, God tell us to have the same personality in us as we follow him.

- Jesus as high as he was, he never praises himself, instead he humbled himself and took a form of a servant and God lifted him up and give him a name that is above every other name.
- Jesus was triumph in everything and every area of his life he was a blessed man; We also out to be like him.
- When you are spiritually minded, like Christ you dominate everything in your life, because you have a godly heritage.

Remember you are a partaker of God divine nature. You are in God's likeness, there is something you carry! it is an **anointing** to cause change in everything you do, maybe it is your **business** that doesn't grow well. When you are spiritually minded in that situation you will know what to do because in your Spirit there are answers to every challenge you face in your life. But remember one thing the anointing you carry doesn't work on business only but in everything and every area of your life. Nobody can be spiritual minded without the Holy Spirit in his life, when the Holy Spirit takes full control of your life you will never be the same again. The kind of things you will be thinking about they will be different from others and you will see life in a different way from the rest of the people out there.

Your mind will see things in a different way, you will never approach life the way you used to approached it before. When you look at people you will see them in a different way, you will have mercy on them then to overlook them. To be spiritual minded give you keys to deal will challenges of life and you will never give up in life. You will always connect yourself with God and God will connect you with the right people in your life. To be spiritual minded will open your spiritual eyes to see things before they happen nothing will just happen without you knowing it first from your Spirit.

### *Learn from The Holy SPIRIT*

After your mind is transformed: The Holy Spirit, will revive your soul take out the desire of sin and enlighten your understanding. The Holy Ghost will give you information that will change your character, humanity, integrity, and personality.

God Holy Spirit wants us to learn from him because He is our helper. Let`s look at the word of God and the character of the Holy Spirit.

**(Luke 4:1KJV)" and Jesus full of the Holy Spirit returned from Jordan and was led by the Spirit into the wilderness."**

The first thing the Holy Spirit will do to you is to lead you!

When the Holy Spirit leads you, be aware of the changes that will take place in your life. Your mind will be renewed, through the word of God and your soul will be build up. The Holy Spirit will inspire your life with the truth and increase your knowledge and understanding.

The book of Luke tells us, Jesus was led by the Holy Spirit into the wildness; what the Holy Spirit was doing with Jesus at that moment was life inspiration and dominating negatives thoughts.

So, now understand the character of the Holy Spirit in your life, the word of God will be our reference.

Change is good, and change is needed, the Holy Spirit will make your life sweet in the middle of challenges, anything He provides unto your life is important and necessary for your future.

The Holy Spirit will lead you to be tested so, that your character can be shaped and be inspired in God by faith.

**(John 14:26KJV)" but the comforter, which is the Holy Ghost, whom the father will send in my name, he shall teach you all things, and bring all things to your remembrance, whatsoever I have said unto you."**

The bible gives us details about the **functions** of the Holy Spirit in our life's, with the **assignment** he is given to do in our journey with him.

- The Holy Spirit will vitalize your mortal body.
- Holy Spirit will teach you ways of God and give you keys of the kingdom.
- The Holy Spirit will bring everything into remembrance so, that you don't forget the word of God and the principles of the kingdom of God.

Be inspired by the Holy Spirit, learn from him your life will be productive and influence-able.

Don't depend on human knowledge and understanding, be influenced by the Word of God.

Be active on learning from the Holy Spirit, never reason the things of the Spirit with your five senses, because the five senses does not know the ways and principle of God. Human **"intelligence"** does not **acknowledge** the presents of the Holy Spirit and his power.

The Holy Spirit will teach you a correct way to **"conduct"** your speech as you learn from him. Remember what we read from the book of (**Luke 4:1 THE HOLY SPIRIT WILL LEAD YOU**). By allowing the word of God to influence your life, even your speech will be corrected, you will say the right things and correct words to address situations, challenges, and dark forces and not only that but even if you respond to anyone you are talking too in any given time.

Whatsoever you say under the power of the Holy Spirit, will change every area of your life and you will be productive, because your speech is full of power and wisdom. In your mouth empty words will never pros ed, the teacher (Holy Spirit) will direct your tongue.

Let's look into the word of God in the book of (**Proverbs 18:21KJV) death and life are in the power of the tongue: and they that love it shall eat the fruit thereof.**

The is power in your tongue and if you don't use your mouth correctly, you will expanse confusing lifestyle, things will be just upside down; that kind of life should never be the part of you. Remember with our mouths, we create whatsoever we want to see in this life.

If you want to see good days keep your tongue from evil, don't speak bad about anyone even if they did wrong to you.

Most people don't know, the tongue carry anointing. That's why we find many people in bondage, not because of the devil; but because they spoke bad against themselves, and the power in the tongue created whatsoever they said to themselves. Every day, as you walk in the light of God; speak the wisdom of God upon your life, business, family, health, the list is endless.

Your body is a vessel of life, anything you connect with becomes alive; the way we are created is amazing, because we able to transfer life throughout our mouth using words or by getting in contact with objects. We are influential people and we able to conduct anything to realty with our emotions or feelings.

So, be sure to understand the ability you have inside of you, with the capacity of energy you carry within your Spirit. Learn on how to use your energy, control and conduct anything you allow in your life as individual person. You have all the keys in life to open any **door** of carrier, opportunists, in life. Remember, life is not what you see with your physical eyes but, life is what you say with your mouth!

The are many things the Holy Spirit will do in your life if you listen to him. If you listen to the Holy Spirit you can be very rich in gold, wisdom, knowledge, understanding, the list is endless. (Romans 8:26KVJ) *Likewise the Spirit also helpeth our infirmities: for we know not what we should pray for as we ought: but the Spirit itself maketh intercession for us with groanings which cannot be uttered.*

CHAPTER 2

# GUARD YOUR HEART

Your heart generate life into your body system. Our body's get life from the blood cells, all the monocles in blood system transfer life into all the body parts. We able to move because of the blood that follows into our veins, as the heart pump blood through the system. For us to be able to do anything, given to us in any form of an object. We must receive information that we can act upon it, in a form of words.

The information we receive into our hearts is translated into words, that is why we able to understand the instructions, given to us to do!

The blood carries the (DNA) of the instruction given to us. You may receive a message, that information you have receive before any action that need to be taken towards the message, the (DNA) of the message must be translated into words.

Now let's look in to the scriptures and see what God say to us about the heart. And how we should be careful of the information we receive into our hearts, as we are influenced by words we hear every day of our life. Our first scripture we find it in the book of proverbs.

**(Proverbs 4:23KJV) keep thy heart with all diligence; for out of it are the issues of life.**

From the scripture, we understand the instruction given to us and the DNA of the message. The instruction given to us is to keep our hearts, there is a reason why we must keep our hearts. The reason can be, the influence we receive throughout words is powerful; and carry a strong energy to transform any person.

Let's look the meaning of the word (**DILIGENCE**) "combination of carefulness and long-term effort"

We must put effort on keeping our hearts from any harm, from all challenges we face every day. The amazing part is we can keep our hearts with all diligence and faithfulness. To be diligence is not something we do ones or sometimes in life, but it`s everyday lifestyle. To be careful got to be part of your life live by it!

WE LOOKING INTO THE WORD GUARD

To protect from danger; to secure against surprise, attack, or injury; to keep in safety; to defend; to shelter; to shield from surprise or attack; to protect by attendance; to accompany for protection; to care for.

In the heart that is where matters of life take place. We learn from the book of proverbs to KEEP, is a principle or responsibility we out to do every day. Second thing we learn is to be diligent, careful of matters of life; and knowing on how to deal with issues of livening. If you not careful about things of life in your heart, you will be heavily loaded with sorrows. When your heart is full of sorrow sickness take control over your body, emotions, heart, and your mind. Sorrowful heart can make you realize many things, which you never experience before in your life.

In everything you choose to do or decide to do in life, make sure your Spirit is clear in every decision you will take at that present moment and so that the challenges you will be facing in future will never be able to trouble your heart. Be careful and follow the principles of God so, that your lifestyle can impress your creator. As you follow the principles of God, your heart will be at peace and rest. Always stand on the truth which is the word of God don't let weakness to influence your heart. Doubt is a weapon that the "DEVIL" use to block the truth from us make us blind so, that we don't see the plain truth.

### *Fill your heart with love*

Love is everything, any person without love find it difficult to enjoy life. Love gives meaning to life, any person covered by sadness and bitterness he or she does not see the reasons of being alive. Whatsoever a person purses in life, if love is not the centre of everything sorrows of life covers everything with shame.

Love is everything but love alone is not enough. Most times you will find people with everything they need in life and discover that the is something beautiful missing in they are life's which is love!

This proves that material things don't proved any human soul with love, but the word of God is love.

How can a person fill the heart with love?

> First, we need to recognize the love we receive from God in us.

> The second thing that we need to understand is each and every person on planet earth is created out of love.

> Reading the bible put the mind of God in your Spirit and you will be filled with love.

> When you look at nature the beauty of their environment will fill your heart with love.

The bible tells us God is love. Let's look at the scripture in the book of **(1 John 4:7KJV) Beloved, let us love one another: for love is of God; and everyone that loveth is born of God, and knoweth God.**

In the scripture above, we find the instruction given to us by the Holy Spirit throughout JOHN; first we must love one another, the reason we got to love one another is because *GOD IS LOVE AND LOVE IS OF GOD*. Every person that loves is born of God, this indicate that nobody can just give love. For us to love one another we must be born of God; true love is found in God. Many people in life they want love, and fail to understand that God is love and for them to find love they got to be filled with love in they are hearts by God.

**1 JOHN 4:8**

**He that loveth not knoweth not God, for GOD IS LOVE.**

If love doesn't rule over your heart, evil ways and evil thoughts rule inside you heart. The is a way to cast out evil by believing to the son of God JESUS CHRIST.

**For God so loved the world, that he gave his only begotten Son, that whosoever believeth in him should not perish, but have everlasting life. (john3:16KJV)**

our hearts need Christ to fill us with love so, that we can share it among each other.

Now let's look how does love influence us every day and the decisions we take as people. There are stein force that manipulate our emotions and feelings so that we move away from the love of God. Most times challenges are the one playing that role in us blind us from the love we receive from God.

- Now we must understand that love gives life.

- Love keeps emotions content in one place.

- Love gives us direction and focus.

- When love influences your life things become easier for you to do them.

- When your heart is filled with love you will find it easy to reach out to others.

**(Ephesians 3:19KJV) and to know the love of Christ, which passeth knowledge, that ye might be filled with all the fullness of God.**

When you heart is filled with the love of Christ, the fullness of God dwell inside of you. How warder-fully is that the hole heaven inside you. No devil can stand on your way, every where you go the greatness of God will prosper you. The love you carry will influence everything around you and the people will favour you. Any business you get involve into it shall prosper because of love. Keep filling your heart with the love of God, sing songs of praise unto the Lord at all times.

Charity suffereth long, and is kind; love envieth not; Love vaunteth not itself, is not puffed up, Doth not behave itself unseemly, seeketh not her own, is not easily provoked, thinketh no evil; Love rejoiceth not in iniquity, but love rejoiceth in the truth; 1 Corinthians 13:4-6

### *HAVE A RIGHT CHARACTER*

**Your character matters a lot in life** , everything in your life depend on your personality. Everything a person does if the character is not mature that person will never be able to achieve anything good in life. A man's character determine his future, every person on planet earth his or her character is influenced by his or her personality a person have and the information the person carries. Many people in the world want to be loved and cared for!

Base on the information people receive in they are life's it is difficulty to receive love, even if love is given unto them they are characters will blind them to see what is offered in front of them. Your character is the key to your destiny, if you have a bad character: opportunity s will pass you by because your character is not a receiving character. It's important that we understand how the system works with us as individual. Whatsoever you attract in your life, your character and personality influence the things you receive as a person. The information we receive as people, is the one that play's a bigger role in building up a person character. How do we see if the person is having a wrong and bad information in his or her Spirit, we look at the character and behavior, of any individual?

Now let's look to the scripture in the book of ( **Matthew 12:35 A good man out of the good treasure of the heart bringeth forth good things: and an evil man out of the evil treasure bringeth forth evil things.**)

The bible tells us clear about the character of any person, out of a good character the will be good things; and out of an evil character the will be corrupt things.

Most times in life, people with corrupt character they always looking for good things to possess, there is nothing wrong with that; the challenge is the forces behind the person is the problem and the motive controlling the person at that particular time is a big problem.

When your life is not going well, and things are not getting done the way you want them to be done Check your character and the information that controls your emotions. And right there you will find your answer and you have the ability to change your character, and control the information you want to receive in your Spirit, and control your emotions. When you having a good character most times it`s easy to connect yourself with the right people to do business with and opportunity`s they just come looking for you. What influences your character is what will give you life and open doors for you in future.

Submit yourself to God's grace and he will move you to high places and let the word of God influence your character you shall have a godly heritage. When you under the influence of the word of God, your life will have a meaning and God will use you to touch many people turn them to Christ. Nobody have life to himself, but we are here to make a different to each other, we are influential to each other. What I have understood is this nobody can change by his or her own power and ability, to have a good character or behavior. We need the power of God to change us and transform us to have a good behavior and godly character. Keep in mind change does not take place over night, we must work on change renewing our minds on the word of God.

# BE CLEAR ON YOUR SPEECH

In life it`s important to use your speech correctly, be clear with everything you say concerning your life. Don't speak confusing words against yourself such as "I am broke, I am not feeling myself or my life is upside down" such words must not be part of your speech. Always be clear on your speech and know what you should say to yourself at all times even if things are not going well by your side. Learn to control your emotions, feed your feelings with words of power for example "you are not a failure in life lines are failing for you in pleasant places, you have a godly heritage, you are full of life and you are a success."

Such information changes your emotions and feelings to be influenced by the power you have inside you. Remember your speech influence your life and direction you take as person, what control your life is the information you receive into your Spirit that control your emotions and feelings.

The words each every person speaks are words from the knowledge they in the Spirit or flesh.

Words we speak they are spirit and powerful, they carry power to do anything they are sent to do. Remember what you say with your mouth it manifest into the physical world taken from the spiritual world. We bring the spiritual things into the physical world. Your words are spirit and alive.

*Let`s look at the word of God in the book of (**Job 22vs 28KJV**) **Thou shalt also decree a thing, and it shall be established unto thee: and the light shall shine upon thy ways.***

*Now the look at how words influence our life`s everyday, the scripture above tell us how powerful are our words.*

*("decree" A decision taken in a point of court or a decision taken in life changing)*

*You shall decide on something and it shall be established unto you. Here we find the power of decision making and how thing will be done if you make up your mind: If your mind is made up on something the grace of God will shine on your way. It's important to be clear on your mind about the things you need and things you say with your mouth.*

*Let's look at the word of God in the book of **(Proverbs 18vs21KJV) Death and life are in the power of the tongue: and they that love it shall eat the fruit thereof.***

*The above scripture tell us something important, our tongue carry power of life and death. This tell us one thing our words can build us up or destroy us and it's important to be clear on your speech because of the power you carry on your tongue. If you want to see change in your life look at the words you say with your mouth, control your speech using the word of God. When you talk the word of God upon your life things will change and favour you. A person living a confusing life, is because of what he or she says using the power of the tongue.*

*In the book of Job the is something we find which is amazing let's look at it*

***(Job22vs29KJV. When men are cast down, then thou shalt say, There is lifting up; and he shall save the humble person)***

*The scripture above give us a direction we should take using our speech, when everyone is talking about sickness, being broke, being depressed, the list is endless; we talk about health found in Jesus and all the good things God is doing every day of our life's.*

*Everything God created on this planet was created out of "words" and with clear speech. Check something now when you at the shop with the dealership and you looking for a car and the dealer ask you Sir or lady what kind of a car are you looking for then you reply anything cheap, the dealer will take you to anything cheap but the kind of car you want is still not known yet and that can make the dealer to give you anything of any* condition, because of how you where not clear on your speech. But if you ask the dealer to give you a MAZDA 3 2015 model black colour and in good condition then the dealer will give you what you asked for because your speech is clear now from the start.

People go around looking for jobs and they are not sure about the kind of job they want they will go say, I am looking for a job but anything that will keep me way from staying at home that speech is not clear you may not get anything out of that. But if you know what you want then you will become clear on what you want. And the kind of job you need by so, doing you will get what you looking for!

Genesis 1:11KJV and God said, Let the earth bring forth grass, the herb yielding seed, and the fruit tree yielding fruit after his kind, whose seed is in itself, upon the earth: and it was so.

Let's look at the scripture above what God said and how he said it! Here we find out how God used authority over the earth and his speech was clear on what the herbs should carry as they grow, and they have to be able to reproduce themself because of the words God said before bring them forth. Even today we still enjoying the herbs God created in the begging of creation. If God did not command the herbs to carry the seed he was going to recreate the herbs again as people consumed the herbs. When you talk be clear on what you want and the kind of things you want to see.

Whenever you in a challenge it can be pain or you need money just be clear on what you want and all shall be well with you; if you in pain use your mouth tell the pain to go just go pain in the name of Jesus Christ go away from my body never return no more the pain will go; just don't give it attention or look for physical results because the devil will show you things in a wrong way make you think the pain is not gone whole is gone. You don't need to pray for money but you need to receive money from you father God; you go according to GOD riches in glory I have my needs meet up therefor in the name of Jesus Christ I receive my portion of money 5 000 or 500 this is a right way to receive.

## <u>REFRAIN YOUR TONGUE FROM EVIL</u>

Psalms 34:13

**"Keep thy tongue from evil, and thy lips from speaking guile."**

After you have clear your speech, now comes an important part keeping your tongue from speaking evil. Any person with a broken heart can speak evil words, against specific people that hurt him or her.

Pain create anger and anger produce negative thoughts that lead to evil speaking, then wrong information comes to influence the mind and produce negative and evil thoughts that will lead on doing something wrong.

So, the scripture given are above tell us to keep our mouths from speaking evil, and how can we stay away from speaking evil words; and what are the things we need to say and know and things we need to do so, that we don't speak evil words against anyone or even our self's.

◇ First thing we need to check is the information we receive from our emotions.

◇ Second thing we need to do is to control the thoughts comes within our minds.

◇ Last-lee we need to feed pain with happy images and happy moments and good thoughts, this way we will be able to control the spirit of anger.

The best part in life we are given solutions to each and everything we come across in life.

1Peter 3:8 For he that will love life, and see good days, let him refrain his tongue from **evil**, and his lips they speak no **guile**: many people want good life and long days on earth, and most time people expect a lot from life. The is nothing wrong with expecting something from life. The challenge is life does not give anything if you don't use the **tongue** correctly.

Our life's are under the influence of our mouths, we need to be very careful how we talk because whatsoever we say-eth with our mouths it's what we shall receive from life, how you talk it is important because your life is shaped by your own words. Happiness is something people need every day and they go around looking for happiness in life, and the is nothing that will give happiness in this world, God he is the giver of happiness and life unto men kind. What we learn from the scripture above is to keep our lips and tongue away from evil words then we shall see good days.

**Ephesians 4:31 let all bitterness, and wrath, and anger, and clamour, and <u>evil speaking</u>, be put away from you, with all malice:**

From the scripture above we see that evil speaking is something we got to put away, our speech needs to be clear because, our words influence our dally life`s. Evil talks drives out love and kindness in us, nobody can give love with an evil heart. Luke 6:45 A good man out of the good treasure of his heart bring-eth forth that which is good; and an evil man out of the evil treasure of his heart bring-eth forth that which is evil: for of the abundance of heart his mouth speak-eth.

Every person speaks the abundance of his or her heart as the bible tells us, we are able to judge the person on the outside, but your words give us an idea of what kind of person are you in side your heart. Nobody can hid his or her heart, and thoughts. Let God the Holy Sprite be the one that will lead your mouth on what to say unto people and unto yourself, so that you don't say anything against yourself and against the people around you.

## CHAPTER 3
## PLAN YOUR LIFE

Planning is important in our life's, it gives us directions and focus on the things we out to do in life. Success does not just come from no where but it comes to any person that take time to plan for it, and to achieve anything in life each and every person needs to plan and commit him or herself to the plan set up front. Each and every person on planet earth, he or she is here with a purpose and in order for anyone to discover his or her purpose; time for meditation and planning must take course. Any person that does not plan for his or her future life! Such person will never achieve anything or bring out something good within himself.

Now let's look at the scripture in the book of Proverbs.

**'Proverbs 16:9 AMP A man's mind plans his way (as he journeys through life), But the Lord directs his steps and establishes them.'**

On the scripture above we find something beautiful, peace of information with a fact of life. When the bible refer us to "MAN" it does not man as man but it refer to each and every one created in the image of God: A man need to take time to think in his mind and plan his way to anything he wants to achieve as a person. Now the peace of information we find in the scripture above is

Man plans and God direct his steps. If you don't plan your life God will never be able to direct your steps (ways) because you have no plans as a person.

Planning is important in each every person and every direction you want to take in life; without planning nobody can discover his purpose in life, and you will never be able to influence yourself or anything around you. Each person must have plan for the future, such plans are called [long team goals] and we have short team goals and every day goals. As we have years and a year and months and weeks and a week and day`s and the day, our planning also needs to be as so!

Individual must have long team goals and short team goals and every day goals, when a child is born as soon he or she grows up future plans are develops inside him or her, whenever he or she`s been asked a questions about the future he or she have the idea of what she wants to be in future: That idea is long team goal, a long team goal it`s a plan that will influence a child to focus on the future. Short team goals are those things we want to achieve in a year or two years, then we have those plans we want to achieve in months or in a month, weeks or a week. Then we have daily plans, things we want to accomplish in day.

Planning influence our life`s daily and keep us from getting lost in our journey of life. Have a dream and also have a idea and plan towards your dreams and ideas, a dream without an idea is just a dream. Proverbs 3:6KJV ***In all thy ways acknowledge him, and he shall direct thy paths.*** In everything put God first, God will make you great and prospers, you will be productive and glory's in life. The most important thing after you have planned everything you want to do, apply commitment to your plans and workout your plans.

### ***DON'T LOSE FOCUS ON YOUR PLANS***

Most people in life plan things and lose focus if they don't see results on what they have planned. After you have set a plan you need to apply necessary tools of life to make the plan work out. Because they thinking they have done everything they supposed to do, or apply whatsoever they need to apply. The difficult thing to do in life is to give up on what you want and what you planned to do in life. The is something we have to understand as people the plans we sit for ourselves, and desires we have comes from God. Let`s look the scripture in the book of (Jeremiah 29:11KJV) **"for I know the thoughts that I think toward you, saith the LORD, thoughts of peace, and not of evil, to give you an expected end."** The LORD give us a message we should go with it everywhere we go and to live by it every day of our life`s, the scripture above tell us that GOD care for us and HE have good thoughts towards us.

The good thoughts the LORD have about us, he gives them to us so, that they give us motive to life and drive us to search for the real purpose of why we are here on planet earth. All the good ideas we have come from within us given by the Spirit of the LORD in us. Most times in life we find many people have brilliant ideas, and with those ideas they can invent new things in they are life and change things complete and other people lives. The only challenge people come a cross is *executing* the idea with a plan from being just an idea to be a reality.

Ephesians 3:20KJV "Now unto him that is able to do exceeding abundantly above all that we ask or think according to the power that work-eth in us." the is power in human Spirit that is working miracles. God can do anything above what we think or ask abundantly with the power that is within us, if God the father wants to move an idea from one country to another he use man: He does not come himself on this planet called earth to move things or do anything without using people. Now look at this, everything you need in life I mean whatsoever it can be you already got, it`s inside of you. The same power God use in you is the same power that bring everything to pass in your life. The power within your Spirit gives your ideas to influence your life to be greater.

Keeping focus on your plans makes the power in you to give life to your ideas and goals. All the challenges you will face will never be able to discourage you or take you of course!

2 Peter 1:3KJV "**According as his divine power hath given unto us all things that pertain unto life and godliness, through the knowledge of him that hath called us to glory and virtue.**"

Look at the scripture above tell us that we got all things we need in life by his power within us. Knowing God is a privilege in life because your life is full of glory, by just having the knowledge of God. Look at this the knowledge you have about God gives you victory through anything in life by the same power he has given us.

Let the knowledge of God influence your life, by allowing the information about God in your Spirit will give your ideas, and a purpose of life and the knowledge of God will inspire you to keep your eyes on your plans and never lose focus. You will never be a dreamer but you will live your dreams inspired by the power in you. Nobody is born to be a failure in life what people don't have is the knowledge of God and of who they are in reality. Many people don't know the ability they have within themselves, that limits many people from achieving they are dreams and goals in life.

The are many distractions in life from viruses things that take our focus away from our plans and dreams, that's why as a person you must be are wear of such things and stay away from them.

## DON'T LOOK DOWN ON YOURSELF

Many times in life we turn to judge ourselves according to other people opinions and descriptions of who we are; forgetting one thing that we are not who they say we are, we are the image of God made in his likeness, we having the character of God in us and all of the earth.

Words from other people should not give you a description of who you are in life, the **WORD OF GOD** should give you a image of who you are in life: don't let negative opinion to influence your thinking towards your image, character, personality, and your ability as a person.

There is good in each and every person in life, that particular good thing a person have is the one that connect him to the system of this world.

Whenever a person think in his or her mind the must be a good picture within the person thoughts, nobody have a negative image about him or herself in life. What create a negative picture in everyone's mind are negative words we receive from others which are not good at all. Those words influence us to think in a wrong way, paint a corrupt image of who we are wily we are not bad people.

- Be careful of the words you receive on your thoughts.

- When you are alone thinking about your life what kind of image do you paint as a person?

- The picture you have inside of you is the picture from God or people opinions?

- Be careful that you don't limit yourself because of your past mistakes.

Ask yourself this questions so, that you able to check yourself and doing that will help you to correct the image you have about yourself. Don't look down on yourself as long you are on this planet; never doubt who you are and what you can do as a person. When you wake up in the morning just know this it's a new day for new things to happen and don't hold on, to happened yesterday because yesterday is gone. Today is given to you to make new decision have the most out of it! Your future carry a lot of things for you and it needs you to be prepare for it and be ready to receive new things.

When things don't go your way don't blame yourself for anything but build yourself for everything, change negative ideas to positive thoughts. Remember this nobody will change your life beside yourself, and you have the ability to build yourself up or destroy yourself.

In your Spirit there is inspiration for the future, and your yesterday and your past life they don't fit on your tomorrow. How do you respond to your future is important and the way you prepare yourself for the future say a lot about your desire. Any desires you have of good things it's given to you it comes from God.

Psalms 37:4KJV delight thyself also in the LORD; and he shall give thee the desires of thine heart.

God doesn't give anyone a evil and negative desire, every person have a good desire. The instruction given to us from the scripture above is to commit ourselves to God and he shall give us our heart desire. Be influenced by your heart desire, the system of this world will tell you many negatives things about life, don't be a victim of low self-esteem. The world will tell you that without education you will never make it in life, this is a lie because with God all things are possible to him that believe (Mark 9:23) get knowledge and also get understanding, with wisdom you can create many opportunities for yourself.

### *GIVE IT YOUR BEST*

You are responsible for your life, nobody is responsible for your decisions and mistakes you do with your life. Whatsoever you need in life it's up to you to achieve it and learn maintain it!

Every decision you take today is not just for this present moment, your future is depending on what you decide to choose today. In life what stand between a man and his success is his mind; the way you think is how your life will be in future. In order for you to have a good life tomorrow, start now be responsible for yourself and stand for what you believe in as Individual.

Commit yourself and submit yourself to your decisions, make sure you don't fail yourself. Create a platform that will be used by the next coming generations after you. Anything you decide to do in life, make it work don't get involved in anything that will never benefit you. **(Psalms 128:2KJV) "For thou shalt eat the labour of thine hands: happy shalt thou be, and it shall be well with thee."** hard work pays anything that a person does under the sun, it got results there is nothing without profit. There is gladness when you eat what you have worked for, and your heart shalt be filled with joy.

Success is not for everyone and success is not for special people, success is for those who say yes to it! Many people want to be successful but they don't want to work for it, most time people they want short cuts in life they don't want to labour for they are needs. Most times people confuse success with money; you can posses money and fail to posses wealthy.

To be able to posses wealthy first thing any person must do is to posses wisdom and understanding: without this two things in life it's be impossible to be wealthy, know this to make money it's easy but to keep it you need wisdom and understanding.

Don't settle for anything you don't want in life but give it your best and achieve your dreams and goals. Anything you want to do in life make a research about it and have information about that project you want to do, don't get involved in anything that will waste your time and capital.

If you understand what you you want to do, it will be easy for you to increase that project to be bigger. Now look inside your Spirit and check what you have: whatsoever you have is what the LORD will use to elevate you to a different level. Each and every person on planet earth have a gift( talent ) from God and that gift is the one that will server you in future, but there is something you must do in order for your gift to server you in future.

✓ First thing you must do don't hid what you have that is your talent.

✓ The second thing you must do is to grow your talent to maturity.

✓ The other thing you must do is to train your talent.

✓ The last thing you must do give it your best and know this building is never easy.

Influence your talent with your ability and the power you have so, that your talent will influence your life and take you to another level of glory. In life there is no plan A or plan B everything you do make sure you do it right the first time. Study things before you get involved in them because your time and effort you won't again them back again unto your life. You the only person having keys to your future and nobody else is going to be responsible for your destiny, only you can make up your mind to be different from everyone and achieve your dreams and goals. How people think of you doesn't define who you are and people thoughts about you they have no power over your life.

# Chapter 4

## Make your covenant with God and keep it!

God is a covenant keeper, he doesn't turn away from his word. Whatsoever he promised you that he will do in your life be sure it will come to pass. Make your covenant with God and don't lose hope seeing that things are not happening at the time you expect them to happen. Remember everything have it's own time as we have different seasons in a year. So if things don't happen at the particular time you expect them to happen just know it's not yet the right time for them to happen. Before God allows something into your life first thing He {God} checks is your ability and your character if you are fit enough to handle what's coming your way. God will never allow anything to come unto your life to rule you and destroy you.

1 Corinthians 10:13 There hath no temptation taken you but such as is common to man: but God is faithful, who will not suffer you to be tempted above that ye are able; but will with the temptation also make a way to escape, that ye may be abler to bear it.

Let's look at the scripture above, here we find that every challenge a person faces in his or her life is not above him or her ability. Whatsoever challenges you may be facing in your life today are common challenges someone else somewhere was dealing with the same thing as you and this tell us that the is nothing new under the sun all things are the same they just use different ways to challenge us. The temptations are there to build us up to make our characters strong and to make us realize the power and ability we carry. If life doesn't challenge you there is no way you will grow and discover who you are and what you capable off.

The covenant you make with God must not be based on the martial things of this world. All you see today is available for you to possess, you don't need to pray for them but you need to receive them. What kind of covenant you need to do with God:

A.  Any covenant you do with God, people of God must benefit from it.

B.  Your covenant must not be for this season only, but for future generations that will come after you they also need be involve on your covenant with God.

C.  The covenant you make with God must involve others and be able to touch many people lives in the present time.

All the promises of God he have made with our four father's he keep-eth them all, that's why you must understand what is the **covenant** and why is important to keep it and live by it every day of your life. A covenant once is made between two people only death can break it, for example two people agree on building maybe offices, then they do that after the offices are finished to be build-ed up; for that agreement to be broken something must happen, in most cases what will happen is this one person will buy out the other person from the property or death can break the agreement between two people.

After you have made your covenant with God know this the devil is not happy with you and your covenant with God and he will come and fight you with everything he have so, that you feel like you have made a mistake and he will try to destroy everything you touch or plans you wanted to do! When challenges comes your way remember the covenant you made with God and know He will never leave you or forsake you and don't doubt God. All the challenges people face every day they come for one reason to take the word of God out of they are hearts. As you fight the good fight of faith know this that the truth is your shield, without the truth you will never be able to stand and fight against the dark forces.

Take the ***whole Armor of God*** because life is spiritual many people they don't know this but life is spiritual and for us to be able to understand life we need to be SPIRIT FILLED. Most times in life people make covenants with God then brake the covenant they have made with God, after that life turn around wrong things start to happen and everything becomes so difficulty to deal with things begin to be a burden.

Let's look into the scriptures (Ephesians 6:10-11KJV) Finally, my brethren, be strong in the LORD, and in the power of his might. Put on the whole Armour of God, that ye may be able to stand against the wiles of the devil. The first thing we find on the scripture above is the command telling us to be ***strong in the LORD*** if you not strong in the Lord you will never be able to stand for what you believe in and you will never be able to stand for the covenant you have made with the ALMIGHT God. The second thing we find is the warning against the devil, for us to be able to stand against the wiles of the devil, we must put the Armor of God the Armor of God will makes us stand against anything that comes from the devil.

Stand till you see your covenant fulfil don't look at your age or your body but keep your head up high, keep your faith don't dwell in yesterday things on what happened or things you could not change. (Romans 4:20KJV) He staggered not at the promise of God through unbelief; but was strong in faith giving glory to God: the scripture above tell us about the father of faith Abraham, how he never look at his body or the deadness of Sarah's womb but He keep on with faith on the promises of God. Keep all the promises of God and everything shall come to pass unto your life, fight the good fight and keep the faith.

### ***MAKE YOUR VOW'S AND KEEP YOUR VOW'S***

as people we make vows to EACH OTHER and to ALMIGHT GOD it is important to keep your vows and honor your vow. God honor any person that honor his or her vow's and God increase grace to the person that keep his or her vow's. If you turn against your word people will never trust you or relay on you because you not a relabel person and even God will never trust you even if you can give to the poor. If you don't keep your vows the is something you doing to yourself and that will cost you a lot of things in your future.


Most times people don't know this but is a fact of life your future is sharped by your own words, and what you say today is your tomorrow. Remember this the words you speak are a seed and how you plant your seeds it depends on what you say today, don't vow to anyone if you know you will never keep your vows, because if you vow and fail to keep your vows you have destroy your future. We don't know what will happen in future but we have hope of good things and great success, and everything depend on us today on how we plant our seeds and honor our vows.

There are things involved in making vows and when you vow with someone know one thing a vow involves two people and two people need GOD in that vow to make it work and to be a success. What are the things involve in making a vow for example I want to buy a house with double door garage and with a nice backyard before I can buy the house I need to look for it, but the question will be

- Which place do I need the house to be at?

- The next thing will be the surrounding does the surrounding suit me as the individual person?

- The last thing will I be I am comfortable or not in that area where the house is?

All this questions I will be asking myself before I vow and buying the house, because everything must be alien with my vision and purpose of my lifestyle.

When you make a vow you look at the place where you at the present moment and where you want to go in a particular time and which year and season you want to see your vow fulfilled. Nobody makes a vow with empty words holding nothing on his or her hands, any person that makes a vow bring something with himself or herself to put on the table to agree on the vows that they will agree on that day.

I remember something when I was growing up, at school the teacher will ask us learns what we wanted to be when we grow up and we will answer by saying many things such as Doctors, Teachers, police the list is endless. At that time we thought things will just happen we go to school and turn to be whatsoever we wanted to be! What the teacher didn't tell us was to be someone important you have to work hard and commit yourself towards your vision of life.

Agreements, vow's and covenants they carry power to change any situation around, when you make a vow have something with you a gift or anything you can give; don't make a vow with empty hands bringing nothing to the table. Remember the words you speak carry power to do anything they are sent to do, whenever you make a vow don't use foolish words thinking that you will achieve anything good; foolish words work against you not the other way around.

Let's look into the word of God and see how Jacob made his vow before the LORD, *(Genesis 28:20-22KJV) Jacob vowed a vow, saying, if God will be with me, and will keep me in this way that I go , and will give me bread to eat and raiment to put on, So that I come again to my father's house in peace; then shall the LORD be my God: And this stone, which I have set for a pillar, shall be God house; and of all that thou shalt give me I will surely give the tenth unto thee.*

Look at how Jacob he make his vow before the LORD he doesn't have a anything on his hand to give to God but the stone he used as a pillar at night to make his vow.

As Jacob went on his journey the LORD blessed him and increase him, anything he touched with his hands was multiple three times more, the vow He did before the LORD made room for him. Anything you vow with before the LORD if you honest and faithful with what you saying, the LORD will make it to come to pass and you will see favour and grace everywhere you go. Your vow's will influence the people you come across in your life; change start by keeping your words and don't turn on your vow, don't vow on anything if your spirit "doesn't agree" with what you want to say, remember God talk to us through our Spirit and he give us directions into our Spirits. Listen to your spirit before you make a vow.

*When thou vowest a vow unto God, defer not to pay it; for he hath no pleasure in fools: pay that which thou hast vowed. Better is it that thou shouldest not vow, than that thou shouldest vow and not pay. ( Ecclesiastes 5:4-5KVJ)*

<u>*AGREE ON SOMETHING AND KEEP YOUR AGREEMENT*</u>

In everything be honest to yourself before you can be honest on others, if you not honest with yourself you will never be honest with others. Life is a journey there are things you will lose and there are things you will again unto your life. Any agreement in order for it to work, it must start working within the person before it can workout on others. Have a agreement with yourself before you can go and make a agreement with other people, commit yourself to your agreement and be faithful.

Any agreement you make with yourself, know this that you are not alone on it because God is your witness and if you keep your word of your agreement God will see you to it that it's fulfilled. Never think you alone in anything because nobody is alone in life; if people they are not around to support you or hold you by your hand, God is there to support you hold you and give you love.

*"He that is faithful in that which is least is faithful also in much: and he that is unjust in the least is unjust also in much." (Luke 16:10KJV) IF YOU ARE FAITHFUL TO YOUR AGREEMENT,* when you are alone then you can be trusted in much more things you will get yourself involved into as you grow more into the future.

Whenever you enter into a agreement with someone or yourself remember to write it down on book or piece of paper; This will prove that you are in agreement with someone that book or paper you have written the things you and the other person you have agreed with keep the book or paper in a safe place. Before there is agreement between two people there are things that they will have to think about before the agreement is finalized. What are those things that they have to look at and think about?

✓ First of all they will have to look at the conditions of the agreement.

✓ The second thing they will have to look at are the terms of the agreement.

✓ The other things they will have to think about are the requirements of the agreement.

The most common thing they will have to look at is this who will benefiting more in the agreement.

The list mentioned above it's not only the things that can be looked at or observe on agreement. Most times people look at what benefits them than to look at other people feelings and benefits.

In everything a person does on this planet they out to receive a reward of all the things they have done and said to others and themselves. Every agreement you do it works for you or against you, if you break a agreement it will work against you and it will bring sorrow and pain unto your life.

You need to be very careful when you make a agreement, don't just agree on anything without you taking your time to think over that particular agreement. Let's look at what Jesus Christ said about things when we agree on them. The book of (Matthew 18:18KJV) ***verily I say unto you, whatsoever ye shall bind on earth shall be bound in heaven: and whatsoever ye shall loose on earth shall be loose in*** *heaven.* Looking at the scripture above we can see that whatsoever we agree on here on earth even in heaven is so, as we agree here on earth. Whatsoever you loose here on earth even in heaven is loose so, be very very careful that you don't do any mistake of breaking a agreement than to be set free from the agreement you where involved in before. Every covenant, or vow's, or agreements as you bind yourself to any of them and you fail to keep any of them, remember this God also was with you on that covenant, or vow's or agreements you have set yourself to keep them.

Your life is influenced by your agreements you do with people and yourself alone. In life nothing just happens without you knowing it in your Spirit, if you take decisions based on your thinking and your decisions they are not supported by your Spirit, expect different results from what you thinking about and what you want to see because your mind doesn't have answers to anything happening around your life. Every agreement you take must influence you every day of your life and inspire you to be faithful and keep you in focus of the promises you have made unto yourself and others.

### *Look unto your vision*

All things we do as people they are driven by a vision given to us by the LORD, remember we talked about *"COVENANT, VOW'S, AND AGREEMENTS"* the next thing we must have in us is the *vision.* See things with your spiritual eyes and don't limit your vision with the negative things you see around happening. What you see with your spiritual eyes is what will influence your vision to be more clear.

Nevertheless even our own **VOW'S** we do before the LORD and with people we have to keep them and be faithful and never turn against our own words. The vision you have in your heart grows more and more strong influencing you more to do more in life. The *AGREEMENTS* we do before the **LORD** and with people, they shall keep us in track and esteem us every day and influences our motives and our decisions we take every day.

Your vision of life is the one that influences you to make the covenant and vow's you have made and the agreeing on them as you did make your agreement, the agreement you have made before the LORD and with people you made it agreeing to your vision of life for the things you are set to do here on planet earth. A person that makes vow's and covenant is a person with a vision he or she is able to see where people can't see with they physical eyes.

If you have a vision and your vision doesn't influence your decision and your life, this means you not feeding your vision the right information to grow and to inspire you to fight for it!

• When you look at the future what do you see?

• What kind of vision do you have about yourself in the future?

• Whenever you look inside your heart is your vision inspiring you to fight for what you believe in?

• Whenever you go to bed what are your thoughts about the vision you carry within your heart?

Every day ask yourself questions to see if you still holding on to your vision of life, the vision you have inside your heart is been given to you by the Almighty God to give to you direction.

The vision you have is not from your mind because your mind will never be able to give you ideas on how to **grow your vision and grow in your vision** and to become a better person in future. Your Spirit carry the vision that God give to you and makes you to understand why you were created and gives you ways on how to fulfill your **purpose in life.**

Everything that comes from a pour heart gives life to that one person that need healing, or to the person that need wisdom, or to that person that needs conceal. The vision you have comes from a pour heart the **heart of God** and your vision carry power and ability to heal, comfort, proved wisdom, prosperity and the list is endless. Physical eyes cannot see the vision inside your heart but your Spirit is able to see and understand the vision well, for you to know and understand the vision you carry inside your heart you must allow the *SPIRIT OF GOD* to influence your Spirit.

When your Spirit is under the influence of the HOLY SPIRIT you will be able to move in right direction and talk to the right people about what you carry, and your life will be productive and fruitful towards your vision. This remind me of the promise God made with Abraham.

God promised Abram to be a father of many nations before He changed his name to Abraham. The time God made his promise with Abram at that moment, Abram did not have children and Abram believed God and listen to the LORD.

What the LORD did was to give a vision to Abraham and Abraham was to follow the vision given to him by God. Let's look in the bible to the book of (Genesis 12:1-3) Now the LORD had said unto Abram, Get thee of thy country, and from thy kindred, and from thy father's house, unto a land that I will shew thee: and I will make of thee a great nation, and I will bless thee and make thy name great; and thou shalt be a blessing: and I will bless them that bless thee, and curse him that curs-eth thee: and in thee shall all families of the earth be blessed.

The vision was the one that give Abraham hope and courage to listen to the LORD and believe God, the vision of Abraham was alive inside him even if he did not have children he believed in what the LORD told him. The most important thing Abraham did was to see the vision with his Spiritual eyes, and he didn't just believe what the Lord told him but he saw the vision that was given to him.

Even today as you go about life see what the LORD invested in you don't end up only on believing but see the vision with your spiritual eyes, but let the vision to inspire your future. The vision you have in your heart for it to grow, it needs you to feed it with good thoughts and information make research about people who had the same vision and they were able to achieve what was given to them by the LORD God Almighty. If you don't work towards your vision in this generation you into right now, someone else will have the same vision as you, and that person will be the one to overtake you and be the one to bring what you were supposed to bring fort.

Be careful of one thing *time* what you have today is time, your time on this planet is important if you don't use your *'time wisely'* the will be lot of things you will miss out on your time frame, things that you are set to accomplish them in a period of time and you where not able to achieve them and reach out to them in time. Remember a vision comes with time frame on it and when it should be fulfilled and accomplished. That is why everything on earth have it's own time to happen, nothing just happen by chance on this planet.

When you look into your vision what do you see? This is a important question we should ask ourselves every day, when you look in you what do you see? There is something you must see when you look into your vision of life given to you by God. And what you see with your spiritual eyes will be the one to influence you every day and give you hope and inspiration to push for more than what you have accomplished in your life. As far as you can see that is how far you can go with your vision, don't be limited by people opinions and negatives thoughts carry your vision with pride remember it comes from the Lord your God.

### *KEEP CONFESING THE WORD OVER YOUR VISION*

How you talk about your vision is important, because very word you say to people about your vision will work on your vision and give you an increase. Many people in life, if they don't understand the vision they carry within themselves they turn to make wrong decisions and allow the pressure of this life to give them impression of who they are and what they carry.

*When you looking into your vision what do you say to it?*

*What kind of thoughts do you have towards your vision?*

*Are you well inspired about the vision you have about yourself?*

*When you think about your vision do you have good ideas towards your vision?*

*Every day* make time to think about yourself and the vision you carry within yourself and ask yourself questions so, that you can be able to check yourself how far are you from seeing your vision coming to pass in your life. Your mind and thoughts must be in peace with your Spirit, the must not be any division within yourself; your Spirit must influence your mind and thoughts to follow the vision you have inside you. There are different kinds of visions

- *There is night vision- this one is the one take place when you are sleeping, seeing things wile you are sleeping in a form of a dream but not a dream.*

- *Then we find day vision- this one take place during the day most time's you will see something before it occur.*

- *Then the is mind vision- this one it happen every time you meditate on something looking for a solution for a particular subject.*

- *Then we have a life vision- this one is a vision you set for yourself make plans for it and get information about it we call this one a carrier.*

> • *We all have a vision given to us by the Almighty God this vision is in our Spirits it cannot be seen with physical eyes, and it cannot be understood with a carnal mind without the understanding from God, this kind of vision each and every person carry is for nations: And everyone connecting to the vision of God he or she becomes a blessing to nations..*

*The vision you carry needs you to meditate on it day and night think about the power* **YOUR VISION CARRYS.** *Where there is no vision people perish, a city with no vision doesn't grow strong and people on that place have no direction of life. Even to you if you don't have a vision your life will never be stable in a place you at and you don't have any direction of life. To grow your vision write it down and make a list of the things you need to do to carry your vision alive.*

*Speak the word of God over your vision and feed your vision with the* **mind of God** which is the Word of God. The words you speak with your mouth they are spirit and alive they don't go out come back empty, now start speaking life over your vision using the Word of God.

Speak with power and authority don't doubt what you are saying, speak things from your Spirit say things you want to see happening over your vision and how you want them to happen learn to talk to your vision. Lines are fallen unto my vision in pleasant places, I have healthy thoughts about my vision.

The most important thing we should all understand is this, that your vision it carry information about you and where you should be in future. As you confess the Word of God over your vision also your vision speak to you and give you advice on how to do things. What your vision will teach

you is to be able to control your thoughts, speech, and how you should visualize things to have a clear picture for your destiny.

Make time to hear the voice of your vision, and learn to have conservation with your vision; by doing that you building up a good relationship with your vision, remember the vision you carry comes from God and to be able to understand it, your Spirit needs to communicate with your vision and your vision talks straight to your Spirit and helps you to understand the journey ahead of you.

In everything you do don't allow your thoughts to influence your Spirit and give you *'negative motives'* about your vision. Every day be under the influence of the Word of God so, that you will be able to confess life over your vision. When you look into a mirror in the morning the image you see there must not be a image of your physical body: but see the vision that is inside of you on that mirror. Always thank God with the vision He have given unto you and learn to be conscious about what you have in you.

**Confession** *Dear Father, thank you for the consciousness of my vision and the victory, success, and the glory of your Word infusing in me. My vision is a success in the name of Jesus Christ, the vision I carry is prosperous, vibrant, strong and energetic. LORD I thank you, for you the one at work in me both to be willing and to do of your good pleasure. LORD your power in me is active to work the vision out and to bring forth blessings and touch life's today. I declare that my vision is as well watered garden, and it bring forth fruits, in and out of season, because my vision is under the influence of you word O, God.*

*My vision will never be cut short, as I carry it I will play my part and do what I'm supposed to do! No devil will oppresses my vision from coming to pass and doing what is set to do.*

*The challenges I will face because of my vision they are coming to build me up and make me strong for my vision. I am productive and fruitful in my life. My vision is not limited with time and space and I am flying up high with the vision God give unto me. I am moving forward and upwards only.*

## CHAPTER 5

## THE WORD OF GOD WITH WORDS OF POWER

*1 In the beginning was the Word, and the Word was with God, and the Word was God. 2 The same was in the beginning with God. 3 All things were made by him; and without him was not any thing made that was made.*(John 1-13KVJ)

Everything we see with our physical eyes comes from the word spoken by the Almighty God Himself with power and authority. Nothing just created it self the word was spoken to bring everything fort to existence. The beauty we see of nature comes from the word spoken by the Almighty.

Let's look at the meaning of the **WORD** in the dictionary ( The spoken sign of conception or an idea, an articulate or vocal sound, or a combination of articulate and vocal sounds, uttered by human voice, and by custom expressing an idea or ideas, a single component part of human speech or language.)

Now let's look at the scripture above and understand the WORD and the assignment. On this verse the word is Christ and here the bible tell us what is the assignment he does in the "God head" *<u>without him nothing was made that was made'</u>* so we exist because of the word that was spoken by God. The word create things and form things, anything created by the word doesn't change character; it always server its purpose as long it exits. Everything God said let it be even today is still there and doing what was form to do. Look at the sky over the beauty of nature how it give's life to anything connected to it!

We have to understand one thing about the words we speak they carry life and they are spirit, whatsoever you say today it will manifest in your life. Before anything said can work on something else it need to work on the person that saying it, then it goes to produce results of the words said by that person: the reason words have to work in you before they can go and work on a particular object words must carry life and attitude of the character which they are send too do.

Let me make a example if you have a dog and you always play with your dog and you have something to do and your dog wants to play the is way you will address the dog to stop playing that way you will show character and attitude towards the dog with strong sound voice. The dog will hear the sound and see the attitude and understand the you character of the owner at that moment and stop playing; you will never address a dog in a sweet voice and expect the dog to listen to you and obey you, it will never happen like that you need to be on point with the dog.

So let's go back ***"in the beginning was the Word and the Word was with God and the Word was God."*** the Word of God is God: there are things formed and there are things created by the word, the words God spoke in the beginning holds things together even today.

We all know that the planet we are living on it is on space, and nothing holds the planet beside the 'Word of God' so that what was spoken in the beginning of creation can always hold things together and the sun will keep shinning every day and the moon will be always be in the night and there is nobody that goes up to during the day to darken the light so that it can be night or the other way around.

The Word of God holds everything together and influence nature to always reproduce as it was commanded to multiply. In each and every one of us the is that voice that always talk to us and instruct us to do well before man and before God and the is no way a person can do wrong before man and think that he or she can do better before God. The voice we hear is from our conscious and God use our conscious to direct us and deliver a message on our Spirits.

With words we create and form things to existence, I want you to think of something maybe an animal 'dog or a cat" already in your thoughts you have a picture of dog with a cat but someone will have a picture of a big dog and small cat. When I say the dog is black already I give you a colored dog, my words will help you to paint a picture of a black dog. This is an example how words play a big role in our lives and in the universe, with words we create and with words we destroy.

The Word of God hold all things together and even our life's are under the influence of the Word of God which was spoken by God to us. There is message that is been given to you in your Spirit that message comes from God, once you take it and live by it your life is under the influence of the ***word of God and his Power.***

Words make us understand direction, instruction, advice, and commandments. In life for us to be able to build a good character we need the Word of God, the words we ready in the bible will make us to understand the mind of God. The Word of God will give us direction of life and give us advice on how to listen to the voice of the Almighty God. If we as people don't receive instructions on how we should workout things in life we will never be able to do anything. Before we make anything before we create something a plan and instructions will be given for that particular project.

***To know wisdom and instruction; to perceive the words of understanding; (proverbs 1:2KVJ)***

The Word of God proved us with wisdom and understanding, we have to perceive the words of understanding. When the spirit of understanding influences your thoughts, your life becomes completely different and your reasoning will be full of wisdom. "For by thy words thou shalt be justified, and by thy words thou shalt be condemned." only in words a person can be put to condemnation, and only with words a person can be justified. Everything u say with your mouth is important, the power in your words will bring you whatsoever thou say-eth.

This book of the law shall not depart out of thy mouth; but thou shalt meditate therein day and night, that thou ma-yest observe to do according to all that is written therein: for then thou shalt make thy way prosperous, and then thou shalt have good success.(Joshua 1:8KJV) looking at the scripture above we find out that we have to use our mouths to talk the Word of God over our life's, with words we speak we can control situations around to favour us. We have to observe and do according to the Word of God then we shalt make our way prosperous, meditation cast out negative thoughts and bring our minds under the influence of the Word of God.

Many people go around looking for prosperity, they will look for prosperity in jobs or business or anything that deals with money You can have a job and fail to be prosperous and have a business but never be prosperous. if you own things in your life that doesn't mean you are prosperous in life, but having things means God have given you grace to achieve things. Prosperity start from your soul where there is connection of Spirits and where change take place. Prosperity comes from God not anywhere else.

### _Keep the instructions and commandments_

Nobody can obey the LORD with out the Holy Ghost been involved in him or her life, human ability doesn't listen to God and it doesn't want God. If you under the influence of your flesh you will never perceive the things of God and understand the will of God for your life. Human flesh doesn't take instruction and commandments, it's so difficult for human understanding to hear the voice of God and take instruction. The reason why many people fail to pray is one because the body doesn't want God, and without the Holy Spirit nobody can pray because the Holy Spirit is the one that make prayers through you using your body to intercede for others.

All scripture is given by inspiration of God, and is profitable for doctrine, for reproof, for correction, for instruction in righteousness:(2Timothy 3:16KJV) Take note instruction comes from God and the scripture is good profitable for the Gospel of Christ (doctrine) for reproof, for correction ( if you hate to be corrected you hate your life ) for instruction(furnishing with knowledge) in righteousness( right standing with God )

Most times in life instruction doesn't come to suit our emotions and feelings. When you facing challenges and prosecution that's when the LORD gives you instructions on what should do to deal with that particular challenge. Instruction may not be the solution you want or looking for at that particular moment to deal with what you are facing. When you take instruction there is guaranty of life, instructions doesn't come empty with out adding anything good unto your life.

*Instructions come in any form it can be a dream, or a vision, even in words. a wise man take instruction and apply wisdom, "whoso loveth instruction loveth knowledge: but he that hat-eth reproof is brutish." Poverty and shame shall be to him that refuse's instruction; but he that regard-eth reproof shall be honour-ed. Apply thine heart unto instruction, and thine ears to the words of knowledge*

**For the commandment is a lamp; and the law is light; and reproofs of instruction are the way of life: {lamp: or, candle}** Proverbs 6:23KJV The commandment of the LORD is a lamp light this means that when you receiving commandment of the LORD you are receiving the light for your journey. You will never walk in darkness, you shall never miss a step and slip or slide.

Many people want to walk in the light but they don't want the light which is Christ, when you have Christ in your life you will walking in the true light the light of God. Darkness will never be able to cover you or have power over you, remember where the is light the is no darkness.

***Then spake Jesus again unto them, saying, I am the light of the world***: he that follow-eth me shall not walk in darkness, but shall have the light of life (John 8:12KJV) To each and everyone that will follow Jesus Christ shall never walk alone and will never walk in darkness. Christ will increase you in knowledge, wisdom and understanding the light of your life will shine above all men. You will never be behind on this generation, you will be ahead of your generation they will always look up for you. The grace of God will move you from glory to glory you will never be in one level of life.

You will have excellent Spirit when Christ influences your life. All the negatives things of life will challenge you but you will be able to overcome them because of the light of life in you. Your understanding will be enlighten, your eyes of your Spirit will be open and you will be filled with love. The Lord is love and he commanded us to do the same give love from his love, the commandment of the Lord they are not a burden to us. The plan of God about us is to prosper us and give us good healthy; God did not create us to be under the influence of poverty, sickness, struggle, and all the negatives things you can think off.

Traditions and cultures have mislead-ed many people from the truth and they don't have knowledge and wisdom for the truth. Many times culture makes people to run after money and prosperity. Money is a defense and answer to most problem in life, but money is not an answer to everything you need in life because money doesn't buy you life. God he is the one that gives you life.

***If ye keep my commandments, ye shall abide in my love; even as I have kept my Father's commandments, and abide in his love.***[John 15:10KJV] The commandments of the Lord they don't come empty but they have a promise and purpose in them, the is life, love, and rest in the commandments of God.

Nobody can keep the commandments of God without the Holy Spirit in him or her, and nobody can keep the commandments of God but failing to keep his or her father's commandments. How does the commandments of God influences our life's, the commandments help us to understand the mind of God and influence us to know who we are in Christ Jesus, because nobody is born without a purpose in life. The only way to stay in God's love is to keep his commandments, nothing else can make you to stay in God's love. **Let us hear the conclusion of the whole matter; Fear God, and** *keep his commandments: for this is the whole duty of man.* Ecclesiastes 13:12KJV

When you are commanded to do something by the Almighty God, do everything in your ability to do what you are commanded to do; because God will never give you something to do without a purpose. The purpose of the commandments you may not know it at that particular moment but be sure of one thing the commandment is for you and the up coming generation after you. When the Lord command you to give something you love and you feel like 'my whole life I was looking for this now I have it the Lord wants me to give it away' or back. If this is the way you feel then that FEELING it is wrong because the Lord want to bless you more and open more doors for you to get much better things than what you already have at that particular time.

The Lord is always looking for a point of contact to bless you, let's look at the scripture in the book of [2Kings 4:2KJV] Elisha said unto her, what shall I do for thee? tell me, *what hast thou in the house*? And she said, Thane handmaid hath not anything in the house, save a pot of oil. When the Lord open doors for you he will use what you have and God does not look for something you don't have he use anything you have. And it's possible that the Lord will use the one thing you say is your last one just to connect you with more blessing. When you are commanded to do something do it as you are told to do, not because you are looking for blessing but because your life is under the influence of the *Voice of God!*

*Have not I commanded thee? Be strong and of a good courage; be not afraid, neither be thou dismayed: for the LORD thy God is with thee whither-soever thou goest.* {Joshua 1:9KJV} Apply this scripture unto your life this is the Lord, talking to you and giving your instruction on what to do in the journey of life with him. The first thing he wants you to do is to be strong, if you not strong when challenges comes you will never be able to stand against them; the second thing we find is courage, if you not courageous it's easy for you to give up and back-down when things turn against you. The other thing we find is to be afraid: the Lord doesn't deal with people full of fear they will be afraid to take important decisions and necessary steps towards life. The last thing we find is to be [dismayed] the dismayed means to be *'intimidated'* never be intimidated by situations and challenges.

The Lord will give you his laws so, that you live by them; his commandments are the lamp unto your journey. God give us his commandments to direct us from where we are to where he wants us to be in life. In life nothing just happen everything is ordained by God. You may say I have not had good day's I am always facing challenges after challenges nothing work out for me. Then how is that God ordained my life to be this way. Let me tell you something the challenges you are facing today they are there to build up your character and make you strong when you are strong your personality is mature to take any challenge down by the guardians of the Holy Spirit.

For God commanded, saying, Honour thy father and mother: and, He that curseth father or mother, let him die the death.[ Mathew 15:4KJV] let's look at the scripture above we find the commandment with instruction of death: if you don't respect your parents and honour your parents you day's on earth are cut short by God himself. You cannot respect God you don't see with you physical eyes, while you are failing to respect your elders, people you are able to see with your physical eyes every day. Respect goes a long way in life and respect create a room for you unto people and God. Learn to build your life based on respect. Even God use someone with respect and humility don't expect to get respect if you can't give it yourself.

(Psalms 119:98AMP) *Your commandments make me wiser than my enemies, for Your words are always with me.* The commandments of God are full of wisdom and God's words will always be with you because he will write His laws in your heart. One of the ways that will help you to understand the scripture is to meditate upon them day in and night. Let's look on the scripture above, God your commandments make me wiser than my enemies; God made Christ our wisdom and if you have Christ in your life then you have the wisdom of God in you. You don't need the wisdom of this world to influence your life because, you have the wisdom of God in you and the wisdom of God will take you to another level in Life. The commandments of God are life unto your flesh and lamp in our journey.

### *DON'T HOLD AN OFFENCE*

*Then said he unto the disciples, It is impossible but that offence s will come: but woe unto him, through whom they come!* (Luke 17:1KJV) The world we live in have so many things today that can make us to sin before God by not forgiving. It's easy to hold an offence and fail to forgive; an offence move us away from God than to bring us close to God. When you holding on to a offence you grief the **HOLY SPIRIT of GOD.** In this world you will be offended by many people and by things that doesn't go well as planed. Even if you are right if you hold an offence that alone makes you to do wrong before the LORD, be careful don't allow the offence to influence you thoughts: because of one reason the offence make the person to think negative and wrong things.

On the scripture above Jesus tell his disciples that it is impossible to stay without being offended. This tell us we will be offended and the decision we will take after being offended determine our future. Nobody can stand and say I am not easily offended, whole living on this planet called earth. Our human understanding can lie to us tell us things we don't want to hear or see, and normal that is what happens most times. Our flesh feed our thoughts with wrong information that will make us to be offended over things we don't have proof over them and even if they are lies not the truth. *"One of the commandments we been give to do and keep is to love each other"*, if you holding an offence how can you love and do right to others, it's impossible to do right if you are influence by the spirit of offence.

The spirit of offence is very dangerous spirit and it can bland you if you not aware of it! The so many good things happening around you, and for you to see them you must be willing to forgive and move on with life. To be influenced by the spirit of offence you lose yourself and you block so many blessing coming your way. **do I exercise myself, to have always a conscience void of offence toward God, and toward men [Acts 24:16KJV]** we must exercise to avoid offence at all time, and when we are offended we must not hold on to offence yes it's not easy when you looking at it with your eyes of your mind; look at it with your eyes of your Spirit in that way, it will give you more understanding on what to do when you are offended.

In human stand-ed everything is impossible and difficult to be done. In everything, we must not forget something important that a mans ability doesn't have power over the *Spiritual world.*

This knowledge must rule in us, that only the Spiritual world have influence in the physical world. Instead the physical world doesn't have knowledge of what is happening on the Spiritual world, but the Spiritual world knows and have information on what is happening on the physical world. The physical-ed things we see with our eyes they came from the Spiritual world.

To hold any offence move you away from your dreams and goals. You will find it difficult to progress in life and everything you will be doing will take to much time before it can products results.

Not because you are doing something wrong but because of what you holding in your heart. it is working against you and influencing everything you are working on to be slow. And if things are slow they will frustrate you big time and if you are frustrated many things around you they stop following towards you. Then you will struggle to get money, you will always be bitter towards everything, you will never be happy about life itself; you will always have wrong thoughts about people around you, not because they doing something wrong to you but because you under the influence of the spirit of offence.

Don't allow the spirit of offence to influence your life. The spirit of offence comes with many wrong things in your life just for one reason to destroy you and your family and everything the family have worked for in life and everything can disappear like water on the dry ground. The way to get over the spirit of offence is to *forgive,* forgiveness doesn't work on others but it works on you help you to heal from the pain you are feeling in your heart and from the negative thoughts you are thinking towards other people who have hurt you.

Human ability doesn't have forgiveness, forgiveness comes from the Almighty God. If you don't follow God you will never be able to forgive others because forgiveness comes from love, for anyone to be able to forgive he or she must have love in his or her heart that love is Christ. The is no way human understanding can understand how love influence us from all things. Love cover multitude of sins, love gives care, love protect, love embrace, love lift up and love doesn't push down the list is endless. For the word of God to work in your life you need to forgive and love the people of God.

### ***WAITING UPON THE LORD***

Everything we see and touch with our hands today have power and ability to influence anybody on earth with good or bad influence. We must understand this that the power we have inside us is able to make all things work possible and the things we want in life they also need the same power to exists and to be able to function on this planet. With the power and ability you have inside you anything you touch with your hands can increase or get destroyed.

In everything we do in life we need to learn to wait upon the Lord and rest upon God for Christ He is our beginning and thee End. **Without Him we can do nothing** if you wait upon the Lord you shall never be put to shame. When you waiting upon the Lord, your life is under the influence of his word and power. You will never take wrong decisions about your life or get involved in a wrong business or anything bad you that will never work out for you.

Remember this everything on this world *work with time* nothing just happen out of it's time frame for it happen. To wait require lot of patient and time with patients you can achieve a lot in life than what you have already achieved.

Waiting will teach you to be responsible and help you to grow mental. You will never take any decision out of carnal mind. **"Wait on the LORD: be of good courage, and he shall strengthen thine heart: wait, I say, on the LORD."** (Psalms 27:14KJV) when you wait on the Lord you shall be strengthen not on the physical body only but also spiritually. Be of good courage tell yourself no matter what you face you shall stay under the grace of God, challenges will come with everything you can think off; when you know that God have your back nothing will move you from the love of God. Never do a mistake to trust people better than for you to trust in God, remember people have they own challenges too of life.

People they are there to help you but not there to save you. God is everywhere but He doesn't meet people everywhere: when you facing challenges after challenges wait upon the Lord an till He talk to you and tell you what you need to do so that you can overcome the challenges you are facing. Don't let challenges to influences your thoughts and tell you wrong things to do because you will never overcome anything but you shall go deeper and deeper into the problem. Remember this your timing and God's timing are not the same, you always want things to be done now at the present moment but God looks at your heart and your character before He can do anything for you. Just because timing is not the same this doesn't mean move away from God and look for help on other things, anything that doesn't come from God comes from the devil.

*But they that wait upon the LORD shall renew their strength; they shall mount up with wings as eagles; they shall run, and not be weary; and they shall walk, and not faint.* [Isaiah 40:31KJV] Let's look at the scripture above and understand what waiting produces, *but they that wait* this indicate that not every person is waiting upon the Lord, only those who trust and depend on the Lord they wait upon him as He is they are refuge. Each and everyone is standing or waiting upon something he or she believes in, nobody can stand and wait upon the Lord if he or she doesn't believe in God. Now those who wait upon the Lord they shall renew they are strength, they shall fly with wings as eagles, they will run and never get tired, they will walk and not faint. Waiting upon the LORD will never shame you, your enemies will never rejoice over you or your family. I say wait upon the Lord and be encourage that the Lord will see you through.

*The LORD is good unto them that wait for him, to the soul that seeketh him.[Lamentations 3:25KJV]* The Lord is merciful to everyone but many people they don't see the mercy of God, not because God hide His mercy from them no, no. The only thing that hides the mercy of God is the sins of man sin makes people blind from seeing the truth. The other reason why people don't see the mercy of God is because they are driven by they are emotions and senses. Follow God with your heart not with your emotions, because emotions will give you wrong information about life and things you want to do and have in life. The Lord is good to them that wait upon Him and unto the soul that seeketh Him. The way to see the mercy of God is by waiting upon the Lord and seeking Him with a pour heart. When things don't go your way wait upon the Lord to show you away you should go and give you a light on how to go on your journey. The mistake many people do is to give up if they don't see anything happening. Rest in the LORD, and wait patiently for him: fret not thyself because of him who prospereth in his way, because of the man who bringeth wicked devices to pass.

### *THE GRACE OF GOD WILL MOVE YOU*

The grace of God will move you to different levels in life, and grace will influence every door you will go thought in life the will be favour upon your life like never before only if you wait upon the LORD. Grace doesn't work with you ability or with your human understanding and knowledge. the grace of God works by the Holy Spirit. The grace of God can be add unto you through the knowledge of God.

When you life is influenced by the grace of God things become easy for you to get them and obtain. The wisdom of God will open your understanding on how to stay under the grace of God, remember sin is the only thing that can move any person from the grace of God. Now when the wisdom of God open your understanding you will be able to know how to deal will yourself and what your flesh wants. The grace of God will do amazing things for you and your life will be at peace, rest be comforted through the grace of God.

Whatsoever people have today in life it can be good education, houses or cars the list is endless everything come from the ***grace of God.*** Nobody have ability to produce wealthy, if the is anyone you know in life and that person is wealthy it is because of the grace of God, nothing else can make a man wealthy. The grace of God will influence your ideas and vision to be a reality; when the grace of God locate you things turn around to favour you, the grace of God make all things possible for you. ***But thou shall remember the LORD thy God: for it is he that giveth thee power to get wealth, that he may establish his covenant which he sware unto thy fathers, as it is this day. [Deuteronomy 8:18KJV]*** for it is God that giveth thee power to have wealth, the reason God give thee power to have all things you are getting out of life, is because of the covenant God made with Abraham in the book of [Genesis 12:1-3KJV] every child of God is under this covenant, the power and ability we have we have it is from God; this is the grace we sharing today that makes all things possible.

For the LORD God is a sun and shield: the LORD will give grace and glory: no good thing will he withhold from them that walk uprightly. {Psalms 84:11KJV} The Lord will give you grace and glory for his sake, and God doesn't hold anything for his children, if you not getting anything from the Lord check where you stand with God. In the missed of challenges where you don't see away out the grace of God is right the to rescue you and save you from the pain and sorrows. The grace of God works in every area of your life to influence everything concerning your life, the grace of God will influence your business, study's, family, understanding, the list is endless. How can a man receive the grace of God by making Jesus Christ his Lord and sever, the is no other that way any person can receive the grace of God without receiving the Lord Jesus Christ; the word was made flesh that word that was made flesh is Christ the grace of God. The grace of God will influence your speech, the words that will be coming out of mouth will be sweet as honey.

*But grow in grace, and in the knowledge of our Lord and Saviour Jesus Christ. To him be glory both now and for ever. Amen.*[2Peter 3:18KJV}

Don't stay in one level take part and grow in grace and in the knowledge of Him[Lord Jesus Christ] be strong in grace, the more you get to know him the more you will grow in grace. You will grow spiritual and the eyes of your understanding will be enlighten, you will be able to see things before they happen. You will increase in wisdom, ability, and power.

Now therefore, I pray thee, if I have found grace in thy sight, shew me now thy way, that I may know thee, that I may find grace in thy sight: and consider that this nation is thy people.[Exodus 33:13KJV] Now on the scripture above we find Moses praying and asking God to show him his ways so that he can know him[God] more and find grace in his sight. This prayer of Moses can be your prayer today, it's important to know who is God and know his ways so that you can live your life for the **Glory of God.** Remember all things that are created under the sun or in heaven are created for the glory of God. Pray to God and he will give you his grace to move you and elevate you to different dimensions. Many times in life we all want to be high and living well, but we don't want to follow the way's of God so that he give us his grace and elevate us.

But he giveth more grace. Wherefore he saith, God resisteth the proud, but giveth grace unto the humble. [James 4:6KJV] The is something the Lord hate is a proud person, a proud person doesn't not have humility, respect and care, everything he or she does is to show off that he or she can do anything and no one will say anything to him or her. But God give grace to the humble, if you want to know the grace of God how it works look at the humble person who is favoured by God. Remember to be proud is a sign that the devil has taken over that person's heart. The way things are the proud person will work hard for everything the is nothing that will come easy on him or her without putting all the ability and effort he or she have.

**Let us therefore come boldly unto the throne of grace, that we may obtain mercy, and find grace to help in time of need.** [Hebrews 4:16KJV] in everything we need we have to go to the throne of grace so, that we find help in the time of need. When you depend on God, in times of challenges and tribulations the only place you will go too, to find help is the throne of God full of grace to help you in those times. The world can't give you grace to stand in any situation or to any challenge in life, only in the throne of grace where you can find mercy and find grace to help you in the time of need. By the **'Mercy of God'** grace and peace be unto you by Christ Jesus our Lord and sever Amen.

# CHAPTER 6

# BE ONE ACCORD WITH THE WORD OF GOD

The word of God have power to heal, build, transform, and save life's the list is endless. Everything that we see with our naked eyes was created by the word of Go. The word of God is the creator of all the planet was created and darkness was upon the face of the earth and as God created everything he was one accord with his word. Unity is power if God was not united with his word, when he said let be light the light was not going to appear because he was not one accord with his word. The real power comes from unity, if you want to see the Word of God works in your life be with one accord with the word you shall see the hand of God move you from glory to glory. To be in unity makes all things possible in marriage if you not in one accord with your partner, that relationship is bound to fail not because of lack of love, or anything else but because of one reason the is no unity in that marriage.

Unity influence many things in our life, it can be in business, friendships, work relationships, or in our family's the list is endless. If we not united is impossible to be in the same church or have a business together or be in friendship for that matter. To be able to keep the family together the are things that need to be involved, but out of everything unity is the key to keep the family together. In the family of four members if they can't love, care, support each other, that family will never be in one accord to keep the family together, the will be challenges in that family they will never be able to stand and fight the enemy. The enemy in any family is jealous, malice, and all the evil ways of the devil.

Let unity rule in everything you do and make sure you in one accord with the word of God. Remember God is everywhere but he doesn't meet man everywhere the is a place where he will take you so, that you can meet with him and be in one accord with him and know him more and better then the way you know him now. Even God want to be united with man but man don't want to be united with the **creator,** but man want to be united with the system of this world. Fellowship with one another reveals how we have to be in one mind and one spirit, if we not united we can be in one place but we will never be in one mind. If you want to see the hand of God move you to different dimension in a church be in one mind, one spirit, and in one accord with the word of God.

And when the day of Pentecost was fully come, they were all with one accord in one place. {Acts 2:1KJV} Without unity there is nothing we can achieve in life, unity attract things we need in life. We all know about the God head, God the Father, God the Son, and God the Holy Spirit.

In the beginning when God said, Let us make man in our image, after our likeness: and let them have dominion over the fish of the sea, and over the fowl of the air, and over the cattle, and over all the earth, and over every creeping thing that crept upon the earth. [Genesis 1:26KJV] on the scripture above we see that God the father was talking to the Word which is Jesus and the dower of the word which is the Holy Spirit, the unity they have is the one that make all things possible.

Fulfil ye my joy that ye be like minded, having the same love, being of one accord, of one mind. [Philippines 2:2KJV] Be of the same love in unity with the same mind nothing bits that.

God move's when he see unity, he fellowship with people when they are united. ***"Jesus said in my name you shall drive out demons"*** for this statement to come to pass to whosoever is using the name of Jesus Christ must be one accord with Word of God and have fellowship with the Holy Spirit: And if the person that is using the name of Jesus is not united with the name the name will never work the will be no results and results comes when the is unity between the person and the name.

## *FELLOWSHIP WITH THE WORD OF GOD*


It's important to be in fellowship with the Word of God, fellowship open your mind on the word of God better and be in enlighten on your eyes of your understanding. Fellowship is the key to unity with the Father through his word, the Holy Spirit will make you understand the mind of God through the Word. We can have fellowship with the Father through his son Jesus Christ and if we walk in the light, as he is in the light, we have fellowship one with another, and the blood of Jesus Christ his Son cleanseth us from all sin.[1 John 1:7KJV] FELLOWSHIP GOES A LONG WAY. We know that Jesus Christ is the light of man and if we have fellowship with him we will walk in love.

If we don't walk in love then we don't know who is God because God is love, any man that walk in darkness doesn't know the love of God.

Fellowship with the Father the Almighty God create a atmosphere of love, care, peace, unity the list is endless. If we say that we have fellowship with him, and walk in darkness, we lie, and do not have the truth in us. If you love God and you have fellowship with him then you will never walk in darkness, your life will be under the influence of the the word of God, it will be easy for you to have fellowship with God through his Son Jesus Christ. The is one way to have fellowship with God is by his son Jesus Christ, here people can ague with me and say we can have fellowship by prayer, reading the Bible, or by worshiping God. The fact of the truth is without Jesus Christ and the Holy Spirit it's impossible to pray, warship, or ready the Word of God; the Holy Spirit he is the one that give us songs to warship God with and he is the one that makes us to pray "for we know not what we should pray for as we ought: but the Spirit itself maketh intercession for us with groanings which cannot be uttered."

Without the Holy Spirit nobody can bless the Lord. The Holy Spirit makes all things possible for us to take part in the kingdom of God, we able to pray and read the bible because of the Holy Spirit.

How do we fellowship with the word of God, meditation and speaking the word these two are the way's for us to have fellowship with the Word of God. Meditation help us to remember the scriptures and know the scripture by heart, speaking the word can be in a form of confession of the word of God over your life or reminding yourself of who you are in Christ: With authority you can use the word of God to put the devil on his place by talking the word. Remember this book of the law shall not depart out of thy mouth; but thou shalt meditate therein day and night, that thou mayest observe to do according to all that is written therein: for then thou shalt make thy way prosperous, and then thou shalt have good success. Joshua 1:8KJV

You the only person that can build or destroy your life or to create an atmosphere for the word of God to work in your life. No devil in hell is able to destroy any person's life but the person himself using his or her mouth. If there be therefore any consolation in Christ, if any comfort of love, if any fellowship of the Spirit, if any bowels and mercies, that ye be like minded, having the same love, being of one accord, of one mind with Christ Jesus.

### ***HEAR THE VOICE OF GOD IN THE WORD OF GOD***

The bible contain the voice of God, all that is written in the Word of God carry the voice of God. ***All scripture is given by inspiration of God, and is profitable for doctrine, for reproof, for correction, for instruction in righteousness:*** [ 2 Timothy 3:16KJV] in the word of God we find doctrine which is the good news of Jesus Christ, in scripture we find reproof [refutation, confutation, contradiction] all scriptures are good for correction, to put man unto order discipline, all scriptures are good for instruction to give direction, all scriptures are good for righteousness to put man in right standing with God.

Whenever you study the word of God you will hear the voice of God in the scriptures, you may study the word and the Holy Spirit give you revelation of what you are studying. The very same revelation you receive from the Holy Spirit, is the same revelation you will need in the future to turn your life around. Everything we receive from the Lord is ordain for that present moment or the future. What was prophesied in the olden days by the Prophets we see the manifest-ion of it today?

*Therefore whosoever heareth these sayings of mine, and doeth them, I will liken him unto a wise man, which built his house upon a rock:* [Mathew 7:24KJV] An person that hears the saying of Jesus and does them he will be called a wise man, that build his future upon Jesus the rock, don't just hear the word of God without putting it to practice. When you practice the word of God that's where your ears will be open to hear more from the Lord, and you will be able to make your way prosperous. The voice of God will direct you and teach you things you have to do and things you must not do. For any person to hear the voice of God his or her Spirit must be open to hear from God.

How God communicate to us is through our Spirits and if your Spirit is not open you will miss the voice of God and it's easy for the flesh to influence your understanding.

When you let the voice of God to influence your life, you will be able to take good decisions that pertain unto life and you will learn how to control your emotions and feelings.

When your emotions and feelings are under the influence of the voice of God your flesh will never have any power to control your thoughts and vision of life. *Take heed therefore how ye hear: for whosoever hath, to him shall be given; and whosoever hath not, from him shall be taken even that which he seem-eth to have.* {Luke 8:18KJV} be careful how you hear, your hearing is important because what you hear to it more shall be added. Your hearing is important learn to check what you hear because the devil also speaks and say things.

The same way we hear also things speak to us in that same way and we respond to what we hear. The world we living into today speak to us in different way's and the system of this world give's unto us information that can block us from the truth and manipulate our life's if we not under the influence of the word of God. When you listening to your Spirit what is it you are hearing, with the same measure you use is the same measure it shall be added unto you.

Hearing is life, without hearing it's '*not easy for any person to build*' his or her life because the will be lack of information coming towards the person. To him that doesn't hear even what he or she have will be taken away from him. Make sure you hear something so that in what you hear more can be added unto you, remember all things have ways of communication. Don't listen to wrong information that will influence you in a wrong direction, which will take you away from the truth which is the word of God. When you under the influence of the word of God and you give you ear to the word you will hear the voice of God. The are people who are under the word of God but they don't give ears to the voice of God.

Who among you will give ear to this? who will hearken and hear for the time to come?(Isaiah 42:23KJV) Who is willing to listen to God, who will give attention to the voice of God for time has come for man kind to hear the voice of God. When you decide to hearken to the voice of God, you will increase in knowledge, wisdom and understanding. People will do anything to get wisdom, understanding and knowledge, the world doesn't offer those things. Wisdom, knowledge and understanding this things are found in the word of the Lord, when you open your ear to hear the voice of God. "The evil people, which refuse to hear the voice of God, as they walk in they are imagination of their heart, and walk after other gods, to serve them, and to worship them, shall even be as this girdle, which is good for nothing."

After you have heard the word what do you do with it! It's important to know what to do with the information we receive because every word spoken to us is God talking to us behind the words we hear the is a voice of God. Be careful of one thing, the devil also knows the scriptures and he can use the word of God to manipulate your intelligence to deceive you. Study the word know the word by your heart and know the voice of God, and know the way God speaks to you using his word.

Don't take chances the devil can pretend to be God and use the scriptures to rob you the glory of God, that is why you need to be careful on how you hear so, that you don't go and do wrong things believing it is God who was spoke to you. Any person that will hearken unto the voice of God he or she will be transform from glory to glory, he or she will move from season to season, he or she will never be in sorrows all his or her life; the person that is under the influence of the voice of God will be able to identify the tricks of the devil, before the challenge comes to him or her. In life don't read the bible because you have to read it but read the bible because you hungry to hear the voice of God speaking to you in his word.

When you are challenged in life and you don't know what to do, don't go around looking for solution in the system of this world; instead look unto God to give you the answers to your challenges and God will direct you to his word to give you solutions to what you will be facing.

Many times in life people will go everywhere to get wealthy, and they can end up selling they are souls in exchange of wealthy. The is something that the people of God forget, that in life the wealth of this world doesn't give peace to any man. Any person can be wealthy in life and its important to know where does the wealthy comes from, because even the devil can make any person wealthy but the devil knows how he will use the wealth to destroy the person.

When God gives wealth to any man the wealthy that comes from God doesn't come with sorrows, and pain. When you don't hear the voice of God after you have wealth be careful because wealth also have a voice and it can speak; and when you listen to the voice of wealth you can lose everything in no time, but if you listen to the voice of God you will be able to keep the wealth and maintain your relationship with God. The is a way to hear a voice of God in your Spirit is to make time to hear from God. Learn to make a quiet time for yourself so that you will be able to learn how to control your emotions using the word of God.

## DO WHAT THE WORD OF GOD TELLS YOU

It's important to hear the word of God, but it's a problem to hear it and never do what is written on it. Whensoever you hear the word of God, obey the word because it comes straight from God to you, when you obey the word of God you are obeying God Himself and by that you are building a good relationship between you and God.

God use his word to direct us and give us instructions, correction, judgement, discipline, righteousness and increase the list is endless. All things given to us by the Holy Spirit through the word of God it is profitable for us and if we don't obey the word of God then we don't obey God.

*Observe and hear all these words which I command thee, that it may go well with thee, and with thy children after thee for ever, when thou doest that which is good and right in the sight of the LORD thy God.*{Deuteronomy 12:28KJV} Let's look at the scripture above and we find the instruction given unto us, the first thing we hear about is **Observe** we need to be careful that we observe the WORD OF GOD and the instruction that comes with the word.

The other thing we find is **HEAR,** what is it that you hear when you listening to the word of God. When you open your Spirit and allow the word of God understand who you have allowed to be part of your life. Know this that the word of God is God when you allow the word in your life, you have accepted God to be part of your life. The other thing we find is **WORDS AND COMMAND** the commandments are for us to understand how we should conduct our life's before God. When ever you do the commandments of God it will go well with you and not only with thee but with your family and future generation. But all the benefits of God will come to pass when you do what he tells you to do.

*Jesus answered and said unto him, If a man love me, he will keep my words: and my Father will love him, and we will come unto him, and make our abode with him.* (John 14:23KJV) Most times people clam to love God and they will be disobedient to the word of God. How do you show that you love God, by obeying his word and doing what the word of God tells you to do.

When you do the word of God, Jesus Christ himself and the father [JEHOVAH] they will come and stay with you and stand by you. When you love God you will be able to give to the poor and share your life for the glory of God. Do the word of God and you shall never go wrong, all things will fail unto place for you. The bible tells us to love one another and if we don't love one another then we are far away from doing the will of God. Run away from the evil ways so that you can keep the word of God by faith.

Therefore to him that knoweth to do good, and doeth it not, to him it is sin. [James 4:17KJV] Every person knows how to do good in the world, just because you know how to do good and you don't do it to you it's accounted as sin. Most times as people we use our past experiences of wrong things that have happened to us to stop us from doing good to others. That is where we will be wrong if we use the negative of the past to stop us from doing right before God.

For it is God which worketh in you both to will and to do of his good pleasure. Do all things without murmurings and disputings:

{Philippians 2:13KJV} everything the Lord tells you to do is for his glory, whatsoever you going through today know this that the Lord is dealing with your future, he is not putting you in shame but you shall rejoice in future.

### *CHAPTER 7*

## *FIND WISDOM AND UNDERSTANDING*

In everything you are looking for in life, make sure you look for wisdom and understanding. Any person without wisdom and understanding doesn't know how to approach life. To win the good fight of faith you need wisdom of God and you need to understand the principle of God and his power. if wisdom and knowledge is not the one influencing your life something else will be influencing your life.

*The fear of the LORD is the beginning of wisdom: a good understanding have all they that do his commandments: his praise endureth for ever.* {Psalms 111:10KJV} the fear of the Lord is the beginning of wisdom, if you fear God you are a wise person and you know the will of God and your life is the blessing for nations. Good understanding and teachable heart are possessed by all those who do the will of the LORD.

God proved wisdom to those who fear him and to those who keep his commandments with understanding. If the is a man, here on earth that doesn't not have wisdom, that person doesn't fear God that is why he or she will never walk with dominion. A light shine more unto a person that keep the commandments of the Lord with understanding. The Almighty God add grace to them that fear him and search for wisdom of God. Wisdom will influence your life to do better things and obtain favour with God and men. The wisdom of God is Christ unto us he is our true wisdom.

*How much better is it to get wisdom than gold! and to get understanding rather to be chosen than silver!* [Proverbs 16:16KJV] How better it is to find wisdom than gold, any man can find gold but if he or she doesn't have wisdom, gold can destroy his or her life.

It best to get understanding because you will understand the will of God over your life and in the kingdom of God. For you to see the favour of the Lord upon your life the key is to find wisdom and get understanding. Wisdom will influence your understanding to take right decisions unto life. Wisdom carry power to change any person's heart to fear the Lord, and the commandments of the Lord open the understanding of man.

My mouth shall speak of wisdom; and the meditation of my heart shall be of understanding. {Psalms 49:3KJV} the Lord will fill you with wisdom, and every word you shall speak will be of authority and wisdom. When you give your heart unto the wisdom of God your meditation shall be of good understanding. Be sure that you follow the principles of God and the Lord will reword you with wisdom to fear him and know the things of the Spirit. Whatsoever you shall see is the hand of God moving you from glory to glory.

When wisdom is part of your life there are things you will never do as a person, not that you fail to do them but because wisdom have open your eyes of your understanding to see things that destroy a man life. Nothing in this world will give any person wisdom and a heart of understanding.

*If any of you lack wisdom, let him ask of God, that giveth to all men liberally, and upbraideth not; and it shall be given him.* (James 1:5KJV) let's look at the scripture above what we find is wisdom in words spoken to us by the Holy Spirit. If you looking for wisdom of God look no feather turn back to God and his word that is where you will find wisdom.

*"If any of you lack wisdom, let him ask of God"* when you looking for wisdom go to God because, God he is the one that gives wisdom unto man, no one else can give you wisdom in this world beside God. A man that invest in the kingdom of God invest in himself, with out wisdom and understanding it is impossible to invest in the things of the

Spirit. Understanding is the key to go about life and the things of the kingdom of God and lay your life for the glory of God.

With wisdom and understanding kings rule the earth, no man can move to a higher level without the wisdom of God. Any person can posses information but if the person doesn't understand anything on that information his or her carry's, life will remain the same as if he or she carry's nothing.We have to understand why we need the wisdom of God in our life's and why we have to understand the systems of this world we living into today. The is wisdom of the world and that wisdom doesn't make any person to fear God and understand his ways.

We can have the wisdom of this world and if we have this kind of wisdom doesn't make us to understand the mystery of the kingdom of God. The wisdom of this world doesn't make us to know God. For any person to know God the fear of the Lord need to bean in his or her heart.

*But the wisdom that is from above is first pure, then peaceable, gentle, and easy to be intreated, full of mercy and good fruits, without partiality, and without hypocrisy.* {James 3:17KJV}

God will give you wisdom that is pure, with no sorrow as the one of the world, the wisdom of God carry peace and it's so gentle. Many times in life we fail to understand how wisdom operate in our life's, that is why many people they don't search for wisdom because they don't understand the importance of it. Any person that lack wisdom you will see him or her by being rude to others and he or she doesn't not have the gentle Spirit. Not that the person want's to be rude no, the spirit that rule in him or her will act foolish and he or she will be arrogant person. Wisdom influences any person to know how to treat others, any person that is under the Spirit of wisdom that person whatsoever he or she will do it be out of wisdom. He will never do anything out of ignorant.

*Wisdom resteth in the heart of him that hath understanding: but that which is in the midst of fools is made known.* (Proverbs

14:33KJV) Wisdom it self is wise it doesn't rest in hearts of fools and wisdom is looking for a person with understanding so that it can dwell and rest in a heart of understanding.

Any man that doesn't understand how to keep his or her mouth quiet, a man of many words doesn't know how to put his heart at rest. The person of wisdom is a man of knowledge and know the ways of understanding.

***Wisdom is the principal thing; therefore get wisdom: and with all thy getting get understanding.*** [Proverbs 4:7KJV] Let's look at the scripture above and see why wisdom have to be part of our life's. Wisdom is principal, without wisdom life is difficult and the is no favour of God upon a man without wisdom in his or her life. In all things you can find in life get understanding so that you will be able to know and understand the principal of wisdom. The world is govern by the principal of God and the system of this world is govern by knowledge. If you have wisdom and understanding you will know how to access the minerals resources. Any person with money can lack wisdom on how to increase the money he or she have and to be rich doesn't mean you have wisdom. If you want to know how rich you are check how much wisdom you carry!

### <u>SEARCH FOR KNOWLEDGE AND FOLLOW IT</u>

The Lord is the God of knowledge. No man will follow the Almighty God without knowledge, because you have to know God with revelation and in spirit. For any person to know the principals of God the person needs to find knowledge and know about the principle of God. Knowledge is the key to build yourself up in the ways of the Lord. When a man is under the influence of knowledge, his or her mind is open for instruction and the knowledge of God. With knowledge kings rule the earth and have access to wisdom just by knowledge. ***Wisdom and knowledge is granted unto thee; and I will give thee riches, and wealth, and honour, such as none of the kings have had that have been before thee, neither shall there any after thee*** *have the like*. [2Choroncles 1:12KJV] when a man fear God this are the things he or she will have in life, before he or she pass to glory.

Wisdom and knowledge is given to a man that is after God's heart, everywhere you will go the Lord grace will locate you and lead you unto green pastures. The Lord honour the person that is after knowledge and wisdom, the is no way a man of wisdom and knowledge will live in poverty.

Wisdom and knowledge will give you riches and wealth no because you capable of having wealth and riches but because God honour you, and give you those things so that you don't live your life in shame. Allow knowledge to lead you and make you a wonder, the is nothing good the knowledge of this world can give unto you than to give you pain and sorrows.

*Therefore they say unto God, Depart from us; for we desire not the knowledge of thy ways.* (Job 21:14KJV). Many people in life they don't want God, but they want things that God proved. The system of this world has blinded many people from the truth, most people in this life they hate the wisdom of God: Don't be surprised at the government when you see the system they have put in place to work for the people and the system fail the people who supposed to benefit from it!

The knowledge of this world cannot hold things together. The problem we do as people is to look unto the system of this world to give us things of God. The way people hate the KNOWLEDGE of God, they prefer to use things that will kill them than to get knowledge and the wisdom of God. In life don't refuse knowledge and wisdom, they are the key to your future and they will help u to create doors of opportunities. When a man refuse wisdom and knowledge of God he or she refuse God to be part of his or her life.

*Grace and peace be multiplied unto you through the knowledge of God, and of Jesus our Lord,* [1Peter1:2KJV] Knowledge is power the scripture above tell us something important about the grace of God. The is only one way to increase the grace of God over your life is to get more knowledge about God then grace shall be added unto you. The is nothing that can help any person to increase the grace of God over his or her life, even if you can give to the poor, giving is good but it can't give any man grace. By this we understand that knowledge is the key to many things in life, if your life is under the influence of knowledge you will know how to control your mind and thoughts so, that you produce good results. *For any person to have the knowledge of God in him or her life they need to know the son of God Jesus Christ, knowledge is found in Christ no where Iin the world or to any system of the world.* **(For the weapons of our warfare are not carnal, but mighty through God to the pulling down of strong holds; Casting down imaginations, and every high thing that exalteth itself against the knowledge of God, and bringing into captivity every thought to the obedience of Christ; {imaginations:) {2Corinthinas 10:4KJV}**

### <u>DISCIPLINE YOURSELF</u>

Be a man or a woman of discipline. Many times in life we don't fail to achieve things we want to have as people, but we take long to receive what we have to receive because of lack of discipline. Any person that doesn't have discipline he or she is living a difficulty life. We all pray for different things in life and we all expect God to answer our prayers, the truth is God answer our prayer as we pray and God send a man to deliver the answer to our prayers. God use people, for a nation to be delivered **'God will send a MAN'** to that nation so that he can save the nation to himself for his Glory.

Before you can see your prayer been answered, the is something you must check if you have it in you that is discipline. The reason I am saying this is because of one thing, most people pray for money, cars, houses, jobs the list is endless. All this things if you don't have discipline they can destroy you and make you to lose your relationship with the Lord. Whatsoever you posses in life, material things they have a language they speak if you don't have discipline they can move your focus away from God's love and end up serving them.

Discipline is part of principle if you don't have wisdom and knowledge you will never be able to have discipline. When you have discipline you have the key for the future, let discipline to influence your life and you will be able to make up your mind on the things you have to do!

Discipline will help you to take the right steps towards your future and know the things you must not get yourself involve in them.

When any person is under the influence of discipline, his or her helps they locate him or her in time. Discipline attract favour and grace and life becomes easy, the will be progress in everything you do because of discipline. ***He openeth also their ear to discipline, and commandeth that they return from iniquity.*** (Job 36:10KJV) If God doesn't open you ear to discipline the is no way you can have discipline. When you have discipline, the Lord will tell you to stop doing something that can kill you and you will stop because you know the voice of God, and wisdom and understanding influence your life so it's easy for you to move from one level of glory to another level of glory.

God doesn't give riches and wealth to a person that doesn't not have discipline, if you rich and you don't have discipline within your Spirit what you have will kill you. God doesn't give wealth to a lazy person because the will be no increase in wealth but the person will eat everything and die. Many people they looking for what will kill them then what will make them live and in life search for wisdom and learn to understand the laws of God. If you are a parent and you don't teach your children discipline they will grow up and they will never understand what it take to work with they are hands and they will never understand the principles that govern the system of this world.

If you don't teach your children discipline you are killing them and you are destroying they are future. Remember this children they don't listen to they are parents, but they imitated they are parents, they will never do something that they never seen they elders do.

***Train up a child in the way he should go: and when he is old, he will not depart from it.*** (Proverbs 22:6KJV) Elders teach the children to fear the Lord also to obey and keep the commandments of the Lord. We all have a role to play in our children future let's be responsible elders for generations to come after us and after our kids.

## *LEARN THE WAYS OF GOD*

We are here on this planet with are purpose, the purpose set by God for our life's, and if we don't know the way of God we will have a big problem because we will never discover the purpose of God about our life's. learn the ways of God so that you live by the principle of God not with the knowledge of man. The ways of God are high then the ways of man, and whatsoever the Lord tells you to do it with out doubt. When God tells you to bless someone give with love and don't look what they do with what you have given them. All you do under the sun instructed by the Lord do it with all your power and might.

***As for God, his way is perfect: the word of the LORD is tried: he is a buckler to all those that trust in him.*** {Psalms 18:30KJV} The ways of the Lord THEY ARE PURE AND THEY LEAD TO RIGHTEOUSNESS . The ways of the Lord they are ways of favour, love, care, joy, happiness the list is endless. The Lord he is a shield to those who trust in him and fear him.

For my thoughts are not your thoughts, neither are your ways my ways, saith the LORD. For as the heavens are higher than the earth, so are my ways higher than your ways, and my thoughts than your thoughts. [Isaiah 55:8-9KJV]

Therefore now amend your ways and your doings, and obey the voice of the LORD your God; and the LORD will repent him of the evil that he hath pronounced against you.(Jeremiah 26:13KJV)

We have to look at our ways as people of God, and we need to do good by the site of the Lord. How can the person do good by the site of the Lord, by helping the poor, taking care of your family,

The Lord wants us to obey him at all times, many times in life what makes people to fail in life, is because they don't want to listen to the voice of God and learn God's ways. The sin of man stand against a man and block a person from being successful in life. Sin put a remote control in a man Spirit so, that the person doesn't understand the ways of God.

But if we put away our wrong doings then the Lord is faithful enough to forgive us and remove us from all iniquity. When you know that the devils hold nothing against you, your soul, mind, and body will be in peace because you stand right with God. One of the reasons why the is no growth in many people life's, is because of sin, and doubt. When you are under the influence of the ways of the God you will be a man of **"FAITH not DOUBT."** The is more to a man of faith then the man of fear and doubt. The Lord made known his ways unto man faith and to him or her that learn the ways of the Lord.

*But take diligent heed to do the commandment and the law, which Moses the servant of the LORD charged you, to love the LORD your God, and to walk in all his ways, and to keep his commandments, and to cleave unto him, and to serve him with all your heart and with all your soul.* [Joshua 22:5KJV] Be diligent in the commandments of the lord and his laws. Never think in your life that you will have your own ways before the Lord, because man ways lead to death. The is only one way to know and learn the ways of God, when you diligent love the Lord God with all you have then the Lord will make known his ways unto you.

### *CHAPTER 8*


## *HAVE FAITH IN GOD AND BELIEVE IN GOD*


*Faith is a principle of God unto the way of living, faith is not for God but faith is for us, and we use faith to receive things we need from the Lord. Faith is the key to your victory in this planet without faith the is no way you can be able to stand and **"fight the good fight of faith"***

*Nobody can walk with God without faith, remember nobody has seen God with the physical eyes and if you don't have faith you will never be able to follow him. Anyone that wants to follow God must believe that he (God) exists, because you will never see God with your physical eyes.*

*The only way to see God in your life is by revelation, if you don't have revelation of who GOD is in your life, it will be difficult for you to follow God.*

***But without faith it is impossible to please him: for he that cometh to God must believe that he is, and that he is a rewarder of them that diligently seek him.*** *(Hebrews 11:6KJV) Without faith it is impossible to please God, if a man want to please God he or she must have faith. He or she that goes to God must believe that God is the rewarded of them that believe and seek him. If a man doesn't have faith he or she will never seek after God, but he or she will see for provision not for the provider. Have this principle in you with you and around you have the God kind of faith. When we study the bible we find out that there is no small faith or big faith, faith is faith. What influence your faith? in this world is what hold your life. With the knowledge you have in your capacity what is it that drives your faith to do the things you do today?*

*When you have the God kind of faith your life will be driven by the wisdom of God. When you are influenced by the God kind of faith every decision you will take it will be the decision influenced by wisdom. The* *man that have the God kind of faith will never take decisions beside on emotions and feelings, the wisdom of **God will direct your focus** on the real challenge then to look upon your emotions and feelings to feed your decision. **But thou, O man of God, flee these things; and follow after righteousness, godliness, faith, love, patience, meekness.**{1Timothy 6:11KJV} O you man of God follow after this things **righteousness, godliness, faith, love, patience, meekness.** This are the things we have to seek and build our life's upon.*

*So then faith cometh by hearing, and hearing by the word of God. (Romans 10:17KJV) to any person that need faith, this is the way to grow your faith by listening to the word of the Lord. The key to **"faith is the word of God"** without the word the will be not faith.*

*When you have faith when you speak you will be speaking the will of God unto man of wisdom. Remember **"all things are possible to him that believe"** without faith no one can believe in God even if the person want to believe in God faith is the key to believe. If you want to walk with God in your life have faith and believe in God.*

*Your faith is the one that will heal you move you to different kinds of levels. Your success depend on your faith and believes. The vision you carry about your life if you don't have faith it's impossible for you to achieve anything out of life.*

### *HAVE TEACHABLE SPIRIT*

*Have teachable Spirit, the walk of faith with the Lord is a walk of faith if you don't have teachable Spirit, you will have difficulties of learning the way of the God. When your Spirit is teachable you will add more knowledge unto your life. Knowledge is power that's why the devil fight a person that find understanding, he know that if the person can find understanding the person will seek after wisdom like never before, and the will be nothing he can do to that person to stop him or her. When you have teachable Spirit the Holy Spirit of God will teach you things and the ways of God and impact you with wisdom and power.*

*The Holy Spirit love to influence the person with an open Spirit and teachable heart. When you have a teachable heart the laws of God will be written on top of the table of your heart. The laws of God they are life to those who find them. The laws of God carry healing and power to convert any person to do the will of God. When you have teachable Spirit you will be always under the anointing of the Holy Spirit to be corrected, loved, protected, appreciate, lead, provided the list is endless.*

*__Forasmuch as an excellent spirit, and knowledge, and understanding, interpreting of dreams, and shewing of hard sentences, and dissolving of doubts, were found in the same Daniel, whom the king named Belteshazzar: now let Daniel be called, and he will shew the interpretation.__(Danial 5:12KJV) Daniel was a man of excellent spirit, and he was a man after the wisdom of God. Looking at the scripture above we see that if you have teachable Spirit the Holy Spirit will give you all this things mention on the scripture above. When the Holy Spirit direct your life he will make you the man of understanding, knowledge, wisdom, and you will be the man of peace. If you don't have teachable Spirit the Lord will not work with you until you have teachable Spirit.*

*__He that hath knowledge spareth his words: and a man of understanding is of an excellent spirit.__(Proverbs 17:27KJV) A man of teachable Spirit have knowledge and he or she doesn't speak mush you will be the person of few words. Understanding will influence your life to understand the things of the Spirit. Teach yourself to listen to the knowledge of God, in that way you will add wisdom of God unto yourself and your life will be amazing.*

*Any man that is not teachable he or she is a difficult person to share wisdom and knowledge with because he or she will never understand the information you will be sharing with.*

*Most times we say knowledge is power and the key to access knowledge is to have teachable Spirit. Knowledge will teach you to observe all things and be alert. The Holy Ghost he is the best teacher and whatsoever things he will teach you, he the Holy Ghost will make you to remember them. If the person is have a unteachable Spirit he will be a proud man and the is nothing he or she will learn from other people. Teachable person humble him or herself so that he or she can learn more from others and become great. Information you receive is the one that will elevate your life and make you great have a teachable heart. You are the key to your future and if you want to have a good life learn to appreciate what the Lord have blessed you with and honour the Lord at all time.*

## *HUMBLE YOURSELF*

*"Humble yourself under the mighty hand of God and he shall lift you up" the is no devil that can stand against the person that is influenced by the grace of God. When you are under the the grace of God, life become easy for you and you move from level to level from glory to glory. The is only one way to get the favour of the Lord upon your life, that way is to humble yourself before the Lord. The Lord doesn't walk with proud people. These six things doth the LORD hate: yea, seven are an abomination unto him: A proud look, a lying tongue, and hands that shed innocent blood, An heart that deviseth wicked imaginations, feet that be swift in running to mischief, A false witness that speaketh lies, and he that soweth discord among brethren.[Proverbs 6:16-19KJV]*

*Looking at the scripture above we see the things that the Lord hate, if you want the Lord to walk with you run away from this things. In life don't be influenced by negative and evil ways of the devil.*

*A proud person doesn't know how to treat other people right and such a person think in him or herself is better than others. In the planet there is no one better than others we all the same in the eyes of the Lord. What make us to be different is the way we receive information unto life. The knowledge you carry is the way your life will be and how you will transform your world. A proud person he or she is full of lies, such people they always have a problem with something in others. A proud person can kill you just to save him or herself, even if they don't kill you physical but they will sacrifice you in front of everyone. A proud person is always thinking evil things in her or his heart devising his or her own life. A proud person just because he or she is full of lies will be a false witness.*

*Likewise, ye younger, submit yourselves unto the elder. Yea, all of you be subject one to another, and be clothed with humility: for God resisteth the proud, and giveth grace to the humble.(1 Peter 5:5KJV) what makes the youth of today to die young is because of one reason they don't listen to the elders and they are not submissive.if you not influenced by humility you will take to much time trying to make up your life to be fruitful. When you are under the influence of humility what you supposed to take five years to achieve you will take lease years to achieve it, because grace will influence your helper to allocate you in season.*

*God resisteth the proud but give grace to the humble. If you don't humble yourself in life, life itself got it's own way to humble a person through ignorance. A proud person is very mush ignorance to many things in life and what the person ignore is what will kill him or her. A proud person is always having excuses about everything coming across him or her that is why they always fail. People fail because of the excuses they have in life, that is why they don't grow up in maturity, they always in one level of life they struggle because they don't want to move or take steps of life.*

***When men are cast down, then thou shalt say, There is lifting up; and he shall save the humble person.****(Job 22:29KJV) God save the humble person when man confessing the failing of the economy, you shall say the is a lifting up, the is no failing to the person that is humble under the influence of the grace of God. "Arise, O LORD; O God, lift up thine hand: forget not the humble. A man's pride shall bring him low: but honour shall uphold the humble in spirit."*

## *CHAPTER 9*

## *FORGIVENESS IS EVERYTHING*

*Forgiveness is important, without forgiveness there are things that will never be experience in life, such as love, care, peace the list of good things is endless. What we see today in the world is the love of God, because of what God did for us by giving us his son to die for our sins on the cross. We are forgiven through Jesus Christ, but not everyone is having this forgiveness of sins only those who confess they are sins and* **accept Jesus Christ as they are Lord and server.** *Love is the key to forgiveness without love the is no forgiveness.*

*The love of God towards mankind is the one that made God to forgive us and send his son to die for us and whosoever believe in him may nor perish but have ever lasting life.*

*The Holy Spirit he is the one that express the love of God in our lives, and also the Holy Spirit is the one that convert us to God. The mercy of God is for us to receive forgiveness of sin.* **To the Lord our God belong mercies and forgivenesses, though we have rebelled against him;** *(Denial 9:9KJV) to God the is mercy of forgiveness of sins, we sin as people but the mercy of God reminds us of what the Lord did for us on the cross. Mankind is re-belles against God and the Lord is so patient we us.*

*The is power in forgiveness and that power works when the person ask for forgiveness, anyone that ask for forgiveness the mercy of God work on him or her because he or she have seen the sins he or she have done before the Lord, and the person wants to repent. What block the mercy of God from working on us is the sin and sin blind the person not to see what the Lord have done for us on the cross.* **But there is forgiveness with thee, that thou mayest be feared.** *(Psalms 130:4KJV) The Lord forgives* *anyone that ask for forgiveness and he will for give you so that you can know him better and understand what he wants from you as a person.*

***In whom we have redemption through his blood, the forgiveness of sins, according to the riches of his grace;*** *(Ephesians 1:7KJV) The is redemption of sins in the blood of the Lord Jesus Christ and forgiveness of sins. The grace in every person life and we need to recognize the grace of God over out life, and move with the grace of God. By the blood we are saved and we have internal life through Christ Jesus, without the love of God which is Christ we can't be under the influence of forgiveness. To forgive is everything and to forgive is to forget. The Lord will never remember our sins no more he has forgiven us forgotten what we have done before him.*

### *FORGIVE YOURSELF FROM ALL GUILT*

*Forgiveness is everything and there is peace and rest when your soul doesn't have any guilt. Anyone that have guilt in his or her heart doesn't have peace in his Spirit, and his or her soul is not at rest with the "truth" the spirit of guilt put people in bondage. The spirit of guilt keep people in one level and stop any person from doing the things the person is out to do in life.*

*Guilt is an evil spirit sent by the devil to condemn any person from doing the right thing. The Spirit of guilt will always show any person the things that they are not doing them right, then condemnation will come to deceive the person that he or she is the failure in life.*

*This is what happens to many people in this world, they are influence by the spirit of guilt. That is why we will see many people who doesn't care about what they are doing in life they are conformable with sin or wrong doing.*

*If you don't forgive yourself as God have forgiven you, then your whole life will be influenced by the spirit of guilt and the person influenced by the Spirit of guilt will stay under condemnation. There is power in forgiveness and when you forgive yourself the is nothing the spirit of guilt will hold against your life. When the is nothing you holding In your spirit then you will be at peace and rest in your spirit.*

*Guilt take away happiness, joy, love, care, respect the list is endless, don't condemn yourself because of the past mistakes you have done forgive yourself and live happy.*

*The truth of the matter is this nobody can free you from condemnation you have in your heart but yourself, and from the spirit of guild if you don't forgive yourself, the only way to get away with the spirit of guilt is to forgive yourself.*

*Any person that live under the influence of the spirit of guild that person doesn't appreciate to wake up in the morning and see the day with what the Lord have done for him or her. The spirit of guild blind many people in life so that they don't see the goodness of the Lord. What influence your life and what makes you to be the person you are today? Let forgiveness to influence your life you will experience the grace of God. When you are free from the spirit of guild your walk with God will be easy and fruitful. The Lord wants us to know him and understand his ways and know his laws. If you don't know what the Lord have done for you, on the cross you will never know how to forgive yourself from all guilt.*

*What will make you to be able to forgive yourself is the faith you have in the Lord, and to know the scriptures the word of the Lord will open your understanding. Receive this power of forgiveness and free yourself from all guilt, how can you receive this power of forgiveness by knowing what the Lord as done for you on the cross, by forgiving you of all sins and taking you out of the kingdom of darkness to the kingdom of light. You are no longer under the influence of guilt but you are under the influence of the light of God. Take the word of God into your Spirit and know the Lord by revelation, **you are no more under guilt.***

## <u>FORGIVE PEOPLE WHO HURT YOU</u>

**Then came Peter to him, and said, Lord, how oft shall my brother sin against me, and I forgive him? till seven times? Jesus saith unto him, I say not unto thee, Until seven times: but, Until seventy times**

*seven. (Mathew 18:21-22KJV) The is no excuses over forgiveness. Most times we have a challenge about forgiveness and on the scripture above we find out that no matter how any times we are wronged we have to forgive as the Father God have forgiven us of all sins. Anyone that doesn't forgive doesn't know the Lord, an person that knows God knows how to forgive because forgiveness comes from God and God is the one who he have forgiven us before we can even know him. Whosoever that says he loves God and know God must have the Spirit of forgiveness in him or her.*

*The scripture above tell us that we have to forgive as long the person ask for forgiveness, doesn't matter how many times the person sin against you. The Lord wants us to understand that forgiveness is everything in his kingdom and if we forgive our journey with him will be sweet as honey. Let the Spirit of forgiveness influence your life and be ruled by forgiveness you will never be under the guilt of nu-forgiveness spirit. If you don't forgive then you not willing to move to the next level in life. People who don't forgive they don't know how to love they are always angry over things, and people they always think of the pain that was cost to them years back. People who don't forgive they live they are life through yesterday in the past. The only thing they want to do is to avenge themselves and hurt others.*

*To forgive is an easy thing if you in Christ, our human ability doesn't have power and capacity to forgive anyone even ourselves. Many people want to do things over they a strength and power, the challenge is our human power and strength can't produce anything good, only the grace of God is the one that able us to do things in life, without the grace of God nobody can forgive any person. If you cannot forgive yourself you will never be able to forgive someone else, forgiveness start with you before you can transfer it to someone else.*

*If forgiveness doesn't work on you it will never work on someone else, the reason other things don't work on us is because we want them to work on others before they can work on us. The principle of God Is this let the word work on you before you can take it to others.*

***So likewise shall my heavenly Father do also unto you, if ye from your hearts forgive not every one his brother their trespasses.*** *{Mathew 18:35KJV} If we don't forgive our brother then likewise the Lord will never be able to forgive us. Learn to forgive like God the is nothing better you can do for yourself then to forgive the people who hurt you. Forgiveness must come from your heart not in your mind or your emotions. Forgiveness is not something you will think about but is something your will act upon. "Take heed to yourselves: If thy brother trespass against thee, rebuke him; and if he repent, forgive him." when you forgive someone you are not doing it for them but you are doing it for yourself. When you forgive healing take place in **"your heart body and soul"***

## *CHAPTER 10*

## *PRAYER WITH SUPPLICATION*

*Prayer is important and if we don't pray we don't have communication with the father. Prayer is our way to communicate with God, by prayer we make our supplication knew to God. A man that doesn't pray the is no communication between him and God. To every challenge he or she will face in life, if the person doesn't get the wisdom of God in that challenge he or she will take wrong decisions based on the challenge. When we pray we access the wisdom of God in our Spirit and solutions for all challenges. Human understanding doesn't provide answers to challenges.*

*Make time for prayer, as you make time for other things you do on your daily life. All things have time and seasons, everything on this world is govern by time and place. If you don't make time for prayer the are things you will never understand how they work. **But when ye pray, use not vain repetitions, as the heathen do: for they think that they shall be heard for their much speaking.** (Mathew 6:7KJV) it's not by many words that your prayer will be answered, when you pray don't repeat one and the same thing over and over again. What makes people to repeat many words in prayer is because they don't "believe in they prayer" and they don't believe that the Lord hear them when they pray. When you pray what comes on your mind matters, because the devil can give you **"negative thoughts think about"** while you pray and your mind will be away from what you are praying for!*

*Pray without ceasing. (1 Thessalonians 5:17KJV) the scripture above tell us to pray without ceasing. We should never stop praying no matter what we face in life. What more can separate us from the love of God. Many people think when you pray for many hour you will have to mush power, the truth is power doesn't come from prayer but power comes from the Holy Spirit. As we know many people pray but they don't have power this is the result that power doesn't come from prayer but the from the Holy Ghost.* **I will therefore that men pray every where, lifting up holy hands, without wrath and doubting.** *[1Timothy 2:8KJV]*

*Be careful for nothing; but in every thing by prayer and supplication with thanksgiving let your requests be made known unto God. [Philippians 4:6KJV] let prayer influence your life and you will never take wrong decisions. In prayer make your requests knew to God, and give thinks to God when you pray, don't give attention to the things of this world. The things of this world will take you away from prayer if you give them attention.*

### PRAISE THE LORD IN PRAYER

*The angles of the Lord stand before the throne of God and give praises to the Lord. When we pray we should offer praises to the Lord, prayer is not a place of complains but prayer is the place of praise. When you give praise to the Lord and the is a challenge you are facing at that moment the will be a solution to that challenge at the spot. Praises set you free anyone that is in bondage let him or her learn to give praises to the Lord, he or she will see the power of God work on his or her behalf. God love to be praised and if you are in bondage and the Lord sees what holds you back in praise he will set you free right there as you give him praise. Praise the Lord in prayer with songs of praise, glorify his name with worship.*

*For great is the LORD, and greatly to be praised: he also is to be feared above all gods.(1Chronicles 16:25KJV) the Lord is great and greatly to be praised and the is nothing that can be put equal with the Lord. Any man that doesn't fear the Lord he or she is acting out of ignorance and he or she doesn't have the wisdom of God. The wisdom of God is the one that will* **"teach you praise"** *and prayer, without the wisdom of God we will never fear the Lord. Remember "the fear of the LORD is the beginning of knowledge: but fools despise wisdom and instruction."*

**Praise ye the LORD: for it is good to sing praises unto our God; for it is pleasant; and praise is comely.** *(Psalms 147:1KJV) praise is the* *principle of God and without the principle of praise the is nothing more we can give to the Lord. If we don't praise the Lord in prayer thereis nothing more we have in us that we can offer to the Lord, our offering to the Lord is praise. As mankind let the spirit of praise to influence your life. The devil is against the man of praise he knows what praise do unto the Lord. There is power in praising the Lord and that power you find in praise work in you and for you. It's pleasant for the Lord that we give him praise.*

*Sing praises to God, sing praises: sing praises unto our King, sing praises. (Psalms 47:6KJV) But ye are a chosen generation, a royal priesthood, an holy nation, a peculiar people; that ye should shew forth the praises of him who hath called you out of darkness into his marvellous light. (1Peter 2:6KJV) we are chosen generation to worship God and sing praises to his name for ever, by our works we give glory but by the name of the Lord we sing praise. What make us peculiar nation is because of the praises we sing unto the Lord.*

***For God is the King of all the earth: sing ye praises with understanding.*** *(Psalms 47:7KJV) The Lord is king of all the earth and everything upon the earth, sing praise unto the Lord with understanding not with carnal mind.*


## *WORSHIP GOD IN PRAYER*

*Worship is a principle of prayer, whenever you pray start with worship and at the end of your prayer end with worship. Worship does with praises and that is the way prayer it should be, full of praise and worship. Most people pray but the pray a wrong prayer, if you pray and in your prayer there is no worship and praise that is a wrong prayer. Remember we talked about praise and prayer, we shared why we need to praise God in prayer.*

*So now we are sharing on worship, there is nothing we can offer God, then to worship him and we have to understand one thing without the Holy Ghost the is no way we can worship God. The Holy Ghost is the one that make us to pray, give praise, and worship God, without him the Holy Ghost we can't pray, praise or worship God.*

*With human ability we can't give praise and worship unto God, remember this "For the flesh lusteth against the Spirit, and the Spirit against the flesh: and these are contrary the one to the other: so that ye cannot do the things that ye would" (Galatians 5:17KJV) the is no one on earth does what he or she wants to do because of the flesh and the Spirit. The time has come to those who want to worship God to recieve the Holy Ghost and that time is now. But the hour cometh, and now is, when the true worshippers shall worship the Father in spirit and in truth: for the Father seeketh such to worship him.(John 4:23KJV)*

*This is the hour that every worshiper should be under the influence of the Holy Ghost. God is not pleased with words without the truth, what make the Lord to receive our worship is the Holy Ghost and the truth which is Christ.*

*A true worshiper have the Spirit of God in him or her without the spirit of God there is no worship. When you let the Spirit of worship to influence your heart, you will have peace in you and you will be at peace with people. "God is a Spirit: and they that worship him must worship him in spirit and in truth." I will worship toward thy holy temple, and praise thy name for thy lovingkindness and for thy truth: for thou hast magnified thy word above all thy name.(Psalms 138:2KJV) be willing to go to the holy temple and worship God with other fellow believers, and praise the name of the Lord, worship God for the truth and love-kindness towards you.*

*O come, let us worship and bow down: let us kneel before the LORD our maker. (Psalms 95:6KJV) we are called to worship God and bow down to him and him alone. There are so "many things that will push you to worship them" but don't allow anything to influence you to worship it. The things you possess as a person can have the influence on you to worship them and love them to much more than the Lord your God. When you worship God many things are reviled unto you by the Spirit of God. Give* unto the LORD the glory due unto his name: bring an offering, and come before him: worship the LORD in the beauty of holiness.

### ***PRAYER FOR SALVETION***

*If you would like to receive Jesus Christ as your Lord and Saviour say the following prayer:*

*"O Lord God, I come to you in the name of Jesus Christ. Your word says "...Whosoever shall call upon the name of the Lord shall be saved" (Acts 2:21kjv). I ask Jesus to come into my heart to be the Lord of my life. I receive eternal life into my Spirit and according to Romans 10:9 "That if thou confess with thy mouth the Lord Jesus, and shalt believe in thy heart that God hath raised Him from the dead thou shalt be saved."I declare that I am saved; I am born-again; I am a child of God!*

*I now have Christ dwelling in me, and greater is he that is in me than He that is in the world! (1 John 4:4kjv). I now walk in the consciousness of my new life in Christ Jesus."*

*CONCLUSION*

As I have shared with you the essential requirements to become a person who comprehends the fundamentality of God. A number of people desire to become excellent and extraordinary, but they don't want to follow God's principles. I strongly believed that God have equipped and anointed me to rise up from this perilous time and influence His Kingdom to operate in understating of His will. We are living in times where youths and adults are constrained to focus more on materialism rather than focusing on God.

**(1 John 2:15-17 NIV) "Do not love the world or anything in the world. If anyone loves the world, love for the Father is not in them. For everything in the world — the lust of the flesh, the lust of the eyes, and the pride of life — comes not from the Father but from the world. The world and its desires pass away, but whoever does the will of God lives forever."**

I want to travel the world and inspire people to excel and become extraordinary but following God's principles in order to understand the will of God. I'm talking about. If we cannot develop a proper relationship and intimacy with God the Father, God the Son and God the Holy Spirit. I want to inform you that your life will be mess up and you will never realize how powerful you are if you are busy focusing on unnecessary things.

Therefore, its primary vital to know your value and align your purpose with God's Word. Please do not be caught up with negativity, because it will delay your process of becoming what God has designed you to be. As I will be travelling and sharing great ideas as how to become a person of excellence.

If you are willing to transform your life and receive a prosper assistance as how you should unleash the power of greatness deposited in you. My social–networking sites can be reachable, and I would be glad to hear from you. Thank you so much –"May the Lord bless, you and reveal His Will and purpose for your life as you read this book daily.

Facebook: Author Monaheng

Facebook page: You Are Created for Greatness

Email address: hardbodynelson@gmail.com

WhatsApp number: +27 79 648 9976

Contact number: +27 79 648 9976

### *About the Author*

*Monaheng sello nelson was born in south Africa in a small town called Heidelberg. The place is situated in Gauteng province . nelson have strive a lot in life and went through a number of ordeals while trying to discover his dream and purpose. However, nelson being a security guard did not stop him from dreaming big and pursuing his purpose. Nelson is determined and optimistic, that one day he will become a published Author. If you could ask him about giving up in the process of pursuing his dream and purpose. he understand this quote better "Quitters never wins and winners never Quit." Therefor Nelson is inspired by the Holy Ghost to compile and write the book title "WHAT INFLUENCES YOUR LIFE" and Nelson have another book titled "YOU ARE CREATED FOR GREATNESS"*

www.ingramcontent.com/pod-product-compliance
Lightning Source LLC
Chambersburg PA
CBHW051856130726
47987CB00002B/859